HC

Collected Poems

Also available in Papermac by Karen Gershon

We Came As Children

Collected Poems

KAREN GERSHON

PAPERMAC

Selected Poems published in 1966 by
Victor Gollancz Ltd, London
Legacies and Encounters published in 1972 by
Victor Gollancz Ltd, London
My Daughters, My Sisters published in 1975 by
Victor Gollancz Ltd, London
Coming Back from Babylon published in 1979 by
Victor Gollancz Ltd, London
'Additional Poems' and 'Joshua Poems' first published
in this edition.

This collection published in 1990 by
PAPERMAC
A division of Macmillan Publishers Limited
4 Little Essex Street London WC2R 3LF
and Basingstoke

Associated companies in Auckland, Delhi, Dublin, Gaborone,
Hamburg, Harare, Hong Kong, Johannesburg, Kuala Lumpur,
Lagos, Manzini, Melbourne, Mexico City, Nairobi, New York,
Singapore and Tokyo

ISBN 0-333-51436-X

A CIP catalogue record for this book is available from the British
Library

Photoset by Rowland Phototypesetting Limited
Bury St Edmunds, Suffolk
Printed in Hong Kong

Acknowledgements

The BBC; *The Times Literary Supplement*; *The Listener*; *The Transatlantic Review*; *The Review of English Literature*; *The Twentieth Century*; *The Critical Quarterly*; *The Jewish Quarterly*; *Outposts*; *Tribune*; *The P.E.N. Anthologies* (1963, 1965); *The Borestone Mountain Poetry Awards Anthology of Best Poems of 1963* (1964); *Present-Day English Poetry* (Hart-Davies); *The Spring Anthology*; *The London Magazine*; *Encounter*; *The New York Times* (USA); *The Jerusalem Post* (Israel); *European Judaism*; *Jewish Chronicle*; Sceptre Press; The Keepsake Press; *Pacific Quarterly* (Australia); Penguin Books; Robson Books; Oxford University Press; Virago; Blackie.

Contents

Foreword   1

Selected Poems   5

Legacies and Encounters   57

My Daughters, My Sisters   79

Coming Back from Babylon   111

Additional Poems   143

Joshua Poems   151

Index   163

Foreword

My first poems I made in German. My mother used to say to me, 'How can you make poems in the language in which we are being cursed!' At that time I expected eventually to write in Hebrew. When I came to England, at the age of fifteen, in the winter before the Second World War, I was on my way to what was then called Palestine and knew more Hebrew than English. The war prevented me from going on and after it I discovered that I would be allowed to stay here permanently. By that time this was what I wanted to do: chiefly because I had begun to write in English.

I had been told, repeatedly, that one could make poems only in the language to which one had been born. I learned not to talk about it and to make my poems in secret. When my eldest sister died of purpura in Bristol in 1943, I was between languages; I continue to mourn not only her death but my still-born poems about it. It took another five years or so – it took having a home with husband and child – to give me what felt like an instinctive use of English.

There was nothing in the poems I made then to betray my background, partly because I still had the illusion that it could be outgrown and partly because I could not yet face the truth about it. My first collection was one of three chosen by Edwin Muir for publication in *New Poets 1959* (Eyre & Spottiswoode, 1960). I made those poems because I needed to prove to myself that I could pass as an English language poet; I believe that poems need to be made for their own sake and they are therefore not included in this volume, which is a selection from my four other collections and includes some later, unpublished poems.

The confidence which being published gave me, and the evidently necessary passage of time, brought me to the poem

'I Was Not There'; it unstoppered my ability, such as it was, to make poems about the Holocaust. I thought of the process as lowering a bucket into a well: down went feelings and attitudes and up came words, allowing me to clarify what I was thinking. In search of understanding I returned, briefly, to my home town, twenty-five years after having left it. There I harvested grief and sowed poems.

I had discarded the German romantic tradition, my inheritance, together with its language. My English mentors were the poets of the First World War, especially Wilfred Owen. A style I discovered for myself: an eight-line stanza with movable rhymes or half-rhymes; finding that it suited me, I came to rely on it; I was not interested in technical experimentation. Kate was my childhood name and after 'Kate's Death' I had nothing left to say about the Holocaust.

Naomi was born the year before that visit to Germany. She was my last child but I did not intend her to be that and I don't know why her birth released so many poems, all made within a few weeks. I have never been able to choose my subject.

Few of my experiences have been fertile; my poems tell of my life like diary entries taken at random. I managed to distil into words no more than a fraction of my thoughts and feelings about Israel; I shirked the task. Yet Tony's suicide attempt, which I shirked talking about, made a poem which came to me almost whole.

Having left Israel again, after living for six years in Jerusalem, I consoled myself by metaphorically stepping out of my life – which I did not just then want to think about – back into my people's past, and made poems on biblical themes. Practising seeing God as my ancestors must have seen him, led me to try to see Jesus as they may have done. When I felt that the words were manipulating my thoughts rather than merely drawing them out I stopped. It felt like my own decision but perhaps my well had run dry.

I made my poems in my head and did not write anything down until I had finished with it. They share first place in my life with my children, but they took up too little space. Needing to work with words more than poetry allowed me to do, I wrote prose, mostly novels, the first of them in the summer before I left home and the next two dozen or so to teach myself to write in English. They were unpublishable or at least unpublished and did not matter to me enough to preserve them. Now novel-writing has become important to me and perhaps that is the reason why I have stopped making poems.

I stopped also because my poems met with too much indifference. Perhaps I shall make some more if this should change or once it ceases to matter to me as I approach my death.

Karen Gershon
St Austell, January 1989

Selected Poems

I WAS NOT THERE

The morning they set out from home
I was not there to comfort them
the dawn was innocent with snow
in mockery – it is not true
the dawn was neutral was immune
their shadows threaded it too soon
they were relieved that it had come
I was not there to comfort them

One told me that my father spent
a day in prison long ago
he did not tell me that he went
what difference does it make now
when he set out when he came home
I was not there to comfort him
and now I have no means to know
of what I was kept ignorant

Both my parents died in camps
I was not there to comfort them
I was not there they were alone
my mind refuses to conceive
the life the death they must have known
I must atone because I live
I could not have saved them from death
the ground is neutral underneath

Every child must leave its home
time gathers life impartially
I could have spared them nothing since
I was too young – it is not true

7

they might have lived to succour me
and none shall say in my defence
had I been there to comfort them
it would have made no difference

TIME WHICH HAS MADE RUINS

Time which has made ruins of
many places I have loved
has no power to destroy
what exists in memory
our temple which was burned
stands for ever in my mind
built of substances which can
defy the practices of men

The eternal light which laid
its mercy on my childhood days
and commanded me to be
servant of its mystery
lodged a splinter of its grace
in my consciousness and throws
on the reality I face
a radiance it cannot lose

SONGS IN EXILE

I

In my thoughts I still return
to the town where I was born
and walk along streets that I know
were ruins sixteen years ago
which rebuilt can never be
welcoming and home to me

8

I who have no other home
love my native town with shame
driven by my memories
riven between loyalties
I love the town my exile built
a replica without the guilt

II

Mine were the hillside and the heath
through ignorance and not by right
mine were the castle and in sight
of witnesses the town beneath

Mine was a share in civic pride
mine was through love but not in truth
the German background of my youth
by which as Jew I was denied

III

Where above the houses
the mixed forest rises
marvellous and wild
bird or berry beckons
as the legend quickens
to the captive child

Here by lake and castle
bygone seasons rustle
in a hunting wind
stories once implanted
keep the child enchanted
in the adult mind

I as well have ventured
where the stark uncensured
certainties are green
my life has two sources
two impassioned forces
I was born between

IV

My town lies in a hand of hills
all words have lost their innocence
the valleys which the township fills
possess a natural defence

Fortresses and memorials
heroic shrines of local lore
raise generations to a false
faith in the gloriousness of war

V

In fear and pride I walked alone
as if I were an enemy
and each stone seemed to look at me
there is no rancour in a stone
to me all things were touched with grace
as I walked in my native place

Mine was each aspect of the town
how does one gain possession of
something but through love enough
through love I made it all my own
each street each house each park each tree
stood in relationship to me

On fences and doors
appear symbols of anger
who were humbled by force
by their pride are made stronger

On the malleable mass
the hands of the master
are poised to impose
the mould of disaster

The tentacles grow
their shadows extinguish
the tremors that show
a nation in anguish

In a people at bay
the primitive rages
converge on the Jew
the purge of the ages

VII

Someone is shouting in the town
me you must have compassion on
and no one heeds it none can hear
fear has stopped up every ear
from the hills the echoes call
have compassion on us all

Coursing through the town the shout
is putting hope and honour out
and barbarities advance
on human indifference
fainter and fainter echoes call
have compassion on us all

AFTER AUSCHWITZ

I

I who am descendent from
those who wept in Babylon
and would not sing their songs to be
comforted in captivity
shall be an instrument to sing
of any human suffering
because in times of genocide
survival must be justified

In my blood and in my bones
are traces of past martyrdoms
centuries of victims lie
latent in my memory
self–despair and curse combine
every life and death in mine
nothing serves me to assuage
the agony of our age

II

Since I am what events have made me
the past remains within my reach
the oldest monument is speech
nothing I value shall evade me

Themes of impermanence obsess me
for my redemption I recall
catharses of my life and shall
not let them go unless they bless me

III

Through ill-lit centuries
along unsheltering walls
on the leash of his enemies
the Jew of the ghetto crawls

Now and again the flames
of history indicate
places spectacles names
manifesting Jewish fate

Here and there a Jew lifts
an individual face
a man for the sake of his gifts
damned he stands for his race

IV

Days which are my life to me
are already history
each succeeding generation
has its own preoccupation
German concentration camps
are replaced by nuclear bombs
people must be left to mourn
the grief to which they have been born

None can afford to ignore
events that have gone before
continuously men have died
because Christ was crucified
all barriers are cancelled by
mankind's innate unity
each futile individual
adds momentum to the whole

Claims of my ancestors
are no concern of yours
one grudge against the Jews
is that they must accuse
Auschwitz was long ago
and could not happen now
why spend emotions on
what cannot be undone

Who wants the future must
come to terms with the past
that peoples rise and fall
makes equals of us all
let none claim precedence
for his inheritance
and there shall be no cause
for which men die by force

KADDISH

I

Simple must be the words I use
to commemorate all these
Jews and those who died like Jews
consider when you label them
sick of sad Jewish memories
making emotional demands
'natural victims of strong hands'
that those who killed them did the same

II

It is not just to think them weak
because they stood in line to die
these people were defeated by
a refusal of the mind
to contemplate what men can do
Christ persecuted was a Jew
and when confronted he was meek
and he had left all hope behind

III

It was the greatest wrong of all
to make their dying bestial
so that it is incongruous
to think of them as glorious
I mourn my parents without pride
I see them as their killers did
who by degrading me as well
are beyond death victorious

IV

I will remember truthfully
who they were and how they died
that is the least I must live through
and by it I can serve them still
in memory of them I will
disburden every enemy
only one hurt through them can show
the mercy which they were denied

V

I will endeavour not to hate
the men who tortured and who killed
each of them has been a child
and was at birth immaculate
I will not curse mankind because
men have made concentration camps
a grief like mine is only stilled
by the inborn need to celebrate

VI

Between their ordinary lives
and their endings must have lain
an enviable state of grace
experience does not explain
why people should prefer to face
all agony with every breath
rather than find an easy death
the knowledge of their choice survives

VII

I think of their illusions and
wonder what thoughts they had of God
if they prayed to him as a friend
they could have had no enemy
if suffering of flesh and blood
assures the soul eternal life
why is their death a cause for grief
a reproach to Christianity

VIII

They all kept their identities
I would have known my parents there
as ordinary people who
responded to catastrophes
not as saints and martyrs do
but with surprise that they should bear
their persecution and not cease
till death from being what they were

IX

There is a drawing of a hand
all evolution in its shape
stretching through a wire fence
to a flower growing beyond
out of the play of centuries
in celebration of life grows
this gesture of such innocence
it can almost be called escape

EASTER

I

When Mary walked in Israel
what made the spirit seek her out
judging that such a girl could bear
the savage world its saviour
would one have known her in a crowd
old masters picture her as frail
as if they had not understood
the burden of this motherhood

II

The Christian world commemorates
the crucifixion of a Jew
that old barbarity which grew
to stand for love by means of hate
the first to suffer in the name
of mankind's most ambitious dream
this one frail figure has become
the vein all life must filter through

III

Were I to mourn the death of Christ
by which my neighbours have been saved
whose twenty centuries of grace
have culminated in this age
it would not be revenge of race
for which survival has sufficed
but anger at man that would make me
reject the pride of Calvary

IV

The resurrection which is spring
has fed like pagan rites on blood
the myth was poisoned at the source
primitive minds imagining
heaven and hell to hold the dead
have set the world upon a course
on which the sacred multitude
must save itself through suffering

V

When her son died was Mary proud
because men said that he was God
she who had been his comforter
in childhood must have questioned what
he thought of as his destiny
it could not have astonished her
to hear the martyr calling out
God why have you forsaken me

VI

When Christ was crowned with his defeat
the cross was turned into the sword
of Christianity to guard
men from their nature and the world
he was a victim of man's youth
betrayed by those who made a creed
that symbolises life by death
he has cursed us with God's word

ANNE IN LIFE AND DEATH

I

I saw her contemplating death
and did not dare to intervene
she had conditioned me to watch
humbly without speech or touch
because it was her death not mine
perhaps if I had roused her by
begging her mercy for us both
she would have refused to die

II

To be her sister was my pride
in our German girlhood when
to be myself I was ashamed
she wore her race so that it seemed
a privilege to be a Jew
dark-haired broad-nosed and almond-eyed
she walked through our hostile town
as if homage were her due

III

I think one so rebellious must
improvise a means to stir
animation out of dust
I crave to be her spirit's host
humanity had need of her
within what chaos are we snared
that life can afford to waste
one whom it had so well prepared

IV

When she was twenty-two years old
the seeds of death burst in her blood
a prelude gaudy with sham hope
was all the shabby life she had
she was so arrogant and wild
we thought her chosen from her birth
perhaps she heard the pulse of earth
pursue her when she was a child

V

I think my sister was afraid
she shared my bed before she died
although she hated to be touched
so destitute she needed me
who was to her as ring to crown
she was cut off as if besieged
from common familiarity
and close to me was still alone

VI

My memories of her are praise
since all who have been born must die
that I may mourn her is a grace
what value I have she gave me
while I am living she survives
beloved usurper of my hopes
she captured me where birthright stops
to share her death gave me two lives

THE CHILDREN'S EXODUS

I

It was an ordinary train
travelling across Germany
which gathered and took us away
those who saw us may have thought
that it was for a holiday
not being exiled being taught
to hate what we had loved in vain
brought us lasting injury

II

Our parents let us go
knowing that who stayed must die
but kept the truth from us although
they gave us to reality
did they consider what it meant
to become orphaned and not know
to be emotionally freed
when our childhood seeds were spent

III

When we went out of Germany
carrying six million lives
that was Jewish history
but each child was one refugee
we unlike the Egyptian slaves
were exiled individually
and each in desolation has
created his own wilderness

22

IV

This race-hatred was personal
we were condemned for what we were
no one escaped the ritual
from which we rose inferior
the blood-guilt entered every home
till daily life was a pogrom
we who were there are not the same
as those who have no wreck to share

V

Home is where some know who you are
the rescue was impersonal
it was no one's concern what use
we made of the years given us
one should not ask of children who
find their survival natural
gratitude for being where
ten thousand others have come too

VI

At Dovercourt the winter sea
was like God's mercy vast and wild
a fever to a land-locked child
it seemed fire and cloud to me
the world's blood and my blood were cold
the exiled Jew in me was old
and thoughts of death appalled me less
than knowledge of my loneliness

VII

My mother sold my bed and chair
while I expected to return
yet she had kept me close to her
till I saw our temple burn
it was not for her sake but mine
she knew that I was unripe fruit
and that exile was a blight
against which one prepared in vain

VIII

People at Dovercourt were gay
as if they thought we could forget
our homes in alien play
as if we were not German Jews
but mealtimes were a market place
when sudden visitors could choose
although we were not orphaned yet
a son or daughter by their face

IX

My childhood smoulders in the name
of the town which was my home
all we were became no more
than answers on a questionnaire
at Dovercourt we were taught that
our share of the Jewish fate
had not been left behind but was
the refugee life facing us

A JEW'S CALENDAR

10th November 1938

I

Searching for my father I
ran through the attacking town
and saw in a familiar street
a lorry being filled with Jews
all men and boys we heard that night
would have to emigrate or die
while planned destruction sampled us
my father walked as if immune

II

Traditionally in pogroms
the cantors try to save the scrolls
I record among their names
that of Siegfried Friedemann
who passed unhurt through fire in vain
and singly within sacred walls
matched against twelve Christian men
proved that Jews are cowards false

III

In the white hours of the night
with lorry-loads of petrol cans
they set the synagogue alight
our right of way to German soil
where roots of generations paused
losing identity until
the weeding of the nation caused
this mutilation of its stones

1933

IV

My grandfather who sought to serve
the God and country of his birth
was in age and innocence
made criminal by circumstance
an epoch ended with his death
he had no blessing to bequeath
all he did and all he thought
nineteen thirty-three crossed out

V

One day when I was nine years old
my mother shouted in the street
which I had never heard her do
remember that you are a Jew
it was as if the world were told
that I had lived with a deceit
and all I was or wished to be
that moment took away from me

1935

VI

She came across the playground like
a swan with cygnets in her wake
I am a German girl she said
I had believed that so was I
who claim that all men are the same
are racialists beneath the brain
by such events a Jew is made
he finds a Jew who looks for me

13th December 1938

VII

The town was innocent at dawn
to it it was another day
but long before we went away
it looked at us and cast us out
had it allowed me to belong
I would have nourished it with song
exiled I cannot sing about
what was an ordinary town

VIII

All that was German in us was
exorcised the day we left
the persecution's single gift
granted a second birth to us
Jewish voices are among
the greatest in the German tongue
had I lived in another time
one of them might have been mine

IX

At the station barrier
my mother would not let me go
I thought that I had outgrown her
I did no longer want her love
I was relieved to leave her there
it was her life that paid my fare
to recollect my childhood now
is the only scourge I have

Spring 1945

X

I climbed some stairs to a bare room
in which the Red Cross lists were spread
naming the German Jews not dead
I could not find my parents' names
so glad was I they could not claim
compensation from me for
the martyrdom they had to bear
that I did not grieve for them

13th December 1941

XI

In the third winter of the war
all remaining German Jews
were exiled to the Russian front
for what was called resettlement
my father and my mother went
of that alone I can be sure
to make up the six million whose
murder was anonymous

XII

One told me that my father died
in Riga of a stroke in bed
I cannot know if someone lied
I only know that he is dead
for four years in the first world war
he was a front-line soldier
he thought himself a German Jew
and was nobody's enemy

XIII

Some said that my mother was
sent to Auschwitz where she died
it may be true but I believe
the transport meant did not arrive
but paced the Polish countryside
until the wagon-loads were dead
they killed Jews in so many ways
I know she cannot be alive

June 1963

XIV

Three years after I left home
the journey to their death began
a quarter of a century
has weathered my emotions till
there is no rage or grief in me
only compassion that men use
the holy solitude they feel
to cultivate catastrophes

MY MOTHER

They were not fit to live who died
my mother was not fit to live
I think of her as one released
from age and illness by her death
as one whom pity would not save
I see the skeleton beneath
the appalling tortured Jew
and not the woman whom I knew

As I am now my mother was
when she was summoned to be killed
I cannot mourn her as her child
I have disowned her for life's sake
her hands once hesitant and white
have touched me with the Jewish plague
she is my enemy because
I am burdened with her fate

IN EVERY STREET

In every street I thought of my father and mother
I did not walk there alone when I was a child
without me they must have walked closer to each other
I am nearly their age now and know that they were not old

Where today the heart of the town pumps tramcars and
 buses
every symbol stresses the travellers' freedom of choice
in this bantam metropolis who is concerned what uses
have been found for the buses which transported the Jews

In my native town I cannot walk like a stranger
all that remains to me of my parents is the truth
their death foreshortens as my shadow grows longer
my life has more space for them now than it had in my
    youth

IN THE JEWISH CEMETERY

The dead Jews lie
divided by
the fate of their families
those with survivors have
flowers on their graves
the others have grass

One who is named
on her family's tomb
died in a camp
when she was twenty years old
I envied her as a child
and am ashamed

My mother's only son
died as he was born
him I also mourn
whatever he has been spared
counts as nothing compared
with what he might have done

My grandparents shall have
an evergreen grave
no flowers shall
divide them from those
whom no one now knows
I mourn them all

IN THE PARK

As I walked alone in my home town's loveliest garden
the past I remembered moved further out of my reach
that so much remained made what was lost to me certain
a sole survivor cannot commemorate much

This was no suitable setting for one in mourning
I thought of my dead and felt guilty to be alive
a multiple shadow lay at my feet as a warning
to the past I pledged all I am all I do all I have

How loved I must have been as a child in this Eden
where the perfect are unselfconscious before their fall
by the dead in whose debt I am I felt myself bidden
to celebrate being alive on behalf of them all

PAVEMENTS

The pavements would not let me rest
they urged me on from street to street
houses and gardens led me past
people whose eyes I could not meet
for fear that one would recognise
and know me by my family
and yet I did not feel that I
was walking among enemies

These were the streets in which I was
plundered of my childhood days
along which Jews with yellow stars
walked to be taken to their death

they fitted me like my own clothes
not who I was but what I thought
marked me out as separate
the pavements touched my feet with fears

MONOLOGUE

Now I am glad to be alone
what is unspoken is my own
I do not want to be consoled
because this grief is all I hold
I will not let my parents rest
and I will not be reconciled
I mourn them and I mourn this child
I have returned and I am lost

I have returned and am alone
if life is neutral what has made
the fearful pattern of my own
and are not all who pray afraid
I submit to no deity
the myth is not defendable
I know I am expendable
my master is society

I have returned but not to curse
where if not here am I at home
I care for neither pride not blame
I search the past for my true source
I want to face my parents' fate
I must know that I may forgive
and I will make it matter that
I alone am left alive

FRIDAY NIGHT

I would have joined the Jews of my home town in prayer
not to praise God but to make myself feel I belonged
in my hallowed childhood servitude I was freer
I am shackled by what I have lost to all that has changed

When choir and congregation answered the cantor
my voice was inaudible under the organ-notes
but I was Ruth I was Esther I was at the centre
where the synagogue stood are now offices and flats

To join in traditional singing was all I wanted
to pause for a moment as if I had really come home
I should have suspected the price of what I was granted
without persecution God is not the same

MY FATHER

I search my childhood continually for my father
as I searched the town for him on the day our synagogue
    burned
all my finds are worthless because I cannot know whether
life or make-believe put these fragments into my mind

I can see him only through death but when he was living
he must have been like my sons once young and with hope
confident of his future an adventurer not a victim
he was proud and respected when I was a child on his lap

Of six million Jews every man has the face of my father
I pity mankind because I feel pity for him
he survives in whatever on earth cries out for mercy
but the loss of his personal life is his and mine

RACE

When I returned to my home town
believing that no one would care
who I was and what I thought
it was as if the people caught
an echo of me everywhere
they knew my story by my face
and I who am always alone
became a symbol of my race

Like every living Jew I have
in imagination seen
the gas-chamber the mass-grave
the unknown body which was mine
and found in every German face
behind the mask the mark of Cain
I will not make their thoughts my own
by hating people for their race

IN A TRAM

I felt most alone when I was surrounded by Germans
who would have sent me to Riga twenty-five years ago
I knew of no means by which I might have determined
their real present reaction to meeting a Jew

What distinguishes these who tolerated the slaughter
from people elsewhere whom they seem to resemble so
    much
did they recognise in me a murdered couple's daughter
does their instinct no longer respond to a Jew within reach

People in trams have decided their destination
they would not have broken the threads of their lives for a
   Jew
had they turned upon me I would have felt less forsaken
I meant nothing to them and they mattered so much to me

THE TOWN

I did not want to feel at home
of what importance was the town
my family were driven from
how could I still have thought it mine
I have four children why should I
expend my love on stones and trees
of what significance were these
to have such power over me

As stones and trees absorb the weather
so these had stored my childhood days
and from a million surfaces
gave back my father and my mother
my presence there was dialogue
how could I have refused to answer
when my own crippled childhood broke
from streets and hillsides like a dancer

IN THE WOOD

I kept forgetting that I was a woman of forty
children too young for history may have thought me mad
when I came out of the wood with my hands and shoes
   dirty
and with tears in my eyes walked up and down the road

Yet not for a moment did I walk again in my childhood
the wood did not echo a word all its magic had gone
every path was for me a secret turning to Auschwitz
there were traces of murder under every stone

Nothing German remains that has not been desecrated
beechwood* will now mean for ever a violent place
nature is neutral my own culpable thoughts created
a setting for tragedy where I might have seen peace

THE ATTIC

I only learned about myself
the old man's story was not true
no one in that house hid a Jew
my parents did not hide themselves
my father was a well-known man
he wore his yellow star with pride
and did not think that anyone
so upright had a need to hide

I stood before the attic door
imagining my parents there
but I could not believe that they
would have chosen to live that way
and suddenly confronted with
a real knowledge of their death
it was as if I were a child
and at that moment saw them killed

*The German for 'beechwood' is *Buchenwald*.

What is the use of finding out
what happened while they were alive
I cannot help them now and have
four children to take their place
not for my parents' sake but mine
I have returned to my home town
I am the echo of their shout
the final fragment of their fate

There was about them nothing strange
they had not always been marked out
for many years it seemed as if
theirs were an ordinary life
I remember who they were
before they died they did not change
no foresight no fear of their fate
would have made them seek refuge there

WILHELM HARMS' HOUSE

This house commemorates my father
who built more lastingly than life
they served him well who put together
this substance of his dream as proof
that as a young man he was bold
but I remember him as old
when the only work he had
was drawing tombstones for the dead

This house once bore my father's name
years ago it was scratched out
let them remember to forget
the murdered mind from which it came
does nobody who knew him care

enough for justice to restore
his name on this corrupted stone
since nothing else can be undone

My father lived and died for houses
digging foundations he was shot
that story may be true or not
I think of him among the driven
preserving as if he were Moses
minor sanities between
the camp guards and other men
in memories his name is graven

EXODUS EAST

As a child I was taught that
the exodus from Egypt was
a miracle and not for us
who could not save himself was caught
how many of six million Jews
sought Sinai confronted with
a journey they could not refuse
and faced the desert of their death

In what way were they different
that they were at the mercy of
that fraudulent resettlement
was being human not enough
they were alone they were alone
she was my mother's friend one said
who helped her pack their things and did
all anybody could have done

Whenever I sit in a train
I see my parents in a truck
events in themselves innocent
bring their experiences back
what explains who can explain
in what way Jews are different
that persecutors can ignore
the humanity all share

My mind invents continually
concentration camp scenes for
my parents waiting for their death
it is as if I must explore
all possibilities and match
imagination with the truth
it is as if they cannot die
until my mind is there to watch

From: Chorus Poems

SUICIDE

I am going to bed she said
and drank death from a common cup
and went to sleep till she was dead
her husband by her dying side
felt love and tried to wake her up
at four o'clock her youngest child
climbed on the bed and found her cold
and cried and could not be consoled.

Four children in fourteen years
she bore (one by Caesarean)
they have grown like poplar trees
one miscarriage (her Benjamin)
made its grave beneath her scar
orphaned she was afraid of ties
her children were her enemies
she was a mother pelican

She had no love to give but work
who cares what poems she betrayed
she did not think them worth her life
out of her parents' death she made
trinkets for warding off the dark
nothing she did was enough
what distinguishes her from
other dead except a name

Believing that all faiths deceive
she could not have been helped to live
a Nazi–German childhood grew
Jesus the forbidden fruit
in the comfort of this Jew
she saw in candlelight the flames
of inquisitions and pogroms
and was homesick for defeat

She would not have survived a camp
and could not live with her escape
she made the world her punishment
whenever she thought of the dead
six million took another step
she was ill-made and self-condemned
within an ordinary shape
she hid the rubbish of God's trade

To her children she bequeathed
refugee gold – memories
an apron twenty-eight years old
and other treasured trash which proved
that as a child she had been loved
and grandparents through whom they had
the smoke of Auschwitz blowing wild
and slaves of Egypt in their blood

1941 AND 41

Thinking of her mother who
was killed because she was a Jew
this woman has grown mad with fear
in her forty-second year
believing that she must live through
everything her mother did
she has made hopelessness her guide
and suffering her comforter

Because she left home as a child
she has barely known her mother
now that she has grown as old
heredity has claimed possession
and with fury and compassion
ground her past and life together
till she has become a mould
overflowing with another

EXPERIMENTS WITH GOD

As a child before she knew
what it meant to be a Jew
she thought that God was on her side
when she was starved when she was stoned
deprived of everything she owned
she felt chosen and was proud
but she was without defence
against God's indifference

From the garbage bin of death
she took the evidence to God
growing articulate beneath
her proliferating load
contaminated by decay
she kept the scavengers at bay
with words till she was silenced by
the gas of Auschwitz on God's breath

THE DEAD COME BACK

All day all night the dead come back
look through the window of her life
at the budding of their stake
and think its promise not enough
to pay her with a word or look
while she suffers they are safe
they cannot help her now because
death has made them enemies

Forced to feed with daily thought
roots of childhood which the drought
of her middle age laid bare

how can she love these ghosts who share
sufficiency that shuts her out
living they looked after her
in death they have become a snare
which does not care that she is caught

HOME

The people have got used to her
they have watched her children grow
and behave as if she were
one of them – how can they know
that every time she leaves her home
she is terrified of them
that as a German Jew she sees
them as potential enemies

Because she knows what has been done
to children who were like her own
she cannot think their future safe
her parents must have felt at home
where none cared what became of them
and as a child she must have played
with people who in later life
would have killed her had she stayed

KATE'S DEATH

So girls in legends dressed at dawn
her eagerness was almost joy
how could she who had packed a toy
know that this was where death began
and she would never be sixteen
before her parents found a phrase

she was willing to leave the house
impatient because they were slow

All windows in the town shammed blind
and only Jews *moved* in the streets
flushed from their shallows to be found
their uses in modern black rites
prepared to be the second who
would resist or run away
she took comfort from the crowd
whose shelter carried her aboard

Self-respect is what makes man
she thought she was not one of those
who clawed their skin and soiled their clothes
and screamed for mercy at the dead
what futile childish self she had
the journey swallowed crumb by crumb
as she observed her parents trying
to save her life while they were dying

So German was the Riga weather
that even natives died like Jews
one told her that they shot her father
she thought how earth and flesh must fuse
and could spare pity for the living
who were vulnerable in
the makeshift foxholes of their skin
where dying was their only weapon

Seven months plucked her girlhood to
feather the far side of death
till she was craving for a faith
that would spare her eternity
burned before she was quite dead
she saw God's hand and thought it Cain's

two thousand years of culture made
fertiliser from her bones

Shrunk to one life within all death
what was left of her mother was
sent to Auschwitz to be killed
from one whole human world they chose
as total value one gold tooth
only thoughts remain and change
the image of man as God's child
into something wild and strange

Other Poems

CAIN

Under gigantic trees
through the primeval grass
quarry from hunter flees
where once Eden was
with bemused surprise
grazing cattle raise
their unblinking eyes
as they pass

Now calf and lamb are born
without a keeper
the overripened corn
rots without reaper
unchecked the beasts of prey
are stalking night and day
the nettle and the thorn
are rooting deeper

No path is to be found
the homestead is decayed
there is no human sound
where once the children played
by jungle overgrown
is the forsaken stone
that sanctified the ground
on which the people prayed

The parents are cast out
from God's protection
age has become a drought
without affection
of their two sons bereft
they have no meaning left
in suffering they doubt
mankind's election

Thicket of rambling rose
harbours the brutal stain
where the bland river flows
whitening bones remain
valley and hillside cry
to the unsullied sky
vengeance shall give repose
to the slain

Caught in a single quest
victim and master
forever without rest
are coursing faster
beast and forest bear
the imprint of despair
all things created share
man's disaster

DANES HILL

Remembering the dead
who remain comforted
by ancient ritual
as I walk on Danes Hill

I think of all that ties
men to their ancestors
in sky-scraper and cave
all share one heritage

By any Babylon
how can I fail to mourn
whose generation fills
the world's memorials

The hillside glows with gorse
there is no path across
whispering shadows stir
the quiet evening air

Forsaken centuries
have taken hold of me
and searching for relief
laden me with their grief

SWISS MORNING

(Vierwaldstättersee)

This has to be seen to be imagined again
flamingoes on the mountaintops at dawn
such metaphors obsess my mind in vain
we cannot help each other and are alone

I am on too familiar terms with death
to look at scenery for its own sake
there lies an inverse universe beneath
the immaculate surface of the lake

Futile to love what cannot reciprocate?
We need relationships to give us scale
expend ourselves on all we encounter that
we need not be pitied for being ephemeral

From: Naomi's Book

MY DAUGHTER LOOKS AT ME

My daughter looks at me and smiles
to her I am the source of life
it does not matter that I have
come more than half way to my grave
to her I am a multitude
of fulfilments and of good
she looks at me and is content
and does not wish me different

Others consider what I am
I suffer to be judged by them
my daughter looks at me and does
not find fault with what she knows
she does not question me because
I am the soil in which she grows
she measures her security
by the faith she has in me

I am angry when I see
what life and I have made of me
and mortified to what extent
I am not as I meant to be
I can find nothing to approve
my daughter looks at me with love
and since if I were different
she also would not be the same
makes me content with what I am

EYES

The brightest colour is a baby's eyes
the first part of its body it inhabits
they venture wait and shy away like rabbits
in a monotony of knitted fleece

They ask what is the selfhood what the shore
the boundaries are fluid like the sea's
they imitate the sky's transparency
without revealing what lies at the core

Through them into the future of the child
look guardians from other generations
they are among the natural notations
the most civilised and the most wild

AT ODDS

A baby like a burning-glass
magnifies the faults one has
I cannot help feeling betrayed
when I am inadequate
by this touch of enmity
in one whom I think part of me
relationship is no defence
against such ruthless innocence
one's children prove what one is worth
a daughter is not made at birth

BIRTH

For your sake when I needed them
immediately strangers came
putting all other tasks aside
and so complete was their command
I had no time to understand
that without help you would have died

As kind as was my mother's touch
was the incision of the knife
I do not owe her hands as much
as those that lifted you to life
I did not know that what can kill
could ever be so merciful

How gentle must have been the care
how well they must have guarded me
as I was lying unaware
I have long known people can hate
and did not think that they could be
so tender and considerate

The hands of strangers gave you life
now I can never again feel
as if I were Ishmael
that only solitude is safe
alone we die and while we live
we owe to others what we have

A SONG IN OCTOBER

Because you are in need of me
I love you with humility
you have served as a pruning knife
to cut dead wood out of my life
leaving me wounds from which to grow
how can I not be humble now

Like the three wise kings who came
to the child in Bethlehem
I am ready to renew
at the source my faith in man
I must be humble before you
who gave me pride when I had none

I love you with humility
because your day casts light for me
and like a wind that blowing through
draws music from some barricade
teaches me how to celebrate
my coronation is in you

IN SPITE OF YOUR RICHES

Of course there are moments when I wish myself free
motherhood ages and you will resent my age
I shall still need you when you will no longer need me
in spite of your riches my servitude is my wage

I am committed to you whoever you are
years of my life will receive their weather from you
my care only serves to make you outgrow my care
all I can give you will not be more than your due

THREE WISHES

I think of children with sad eyes
the dead the living the unborn
coins that pay for human choice
whose mothers mourn

I wish for you compassion enough
no cause for grief
and a talent with which to relieve
the dearth of love

NIGHT AND DAY

You need me in the night when each
separately samples death
you still exist submerged beneath
oceans of sleep out of my reach
as bread is to growing corn
you will be to the newly born

I have made you for my sake
but your total scope must be
far more than what touches me
as a spring can make a lake
to give birth is not enough
this is what I am guilty of

You lend direction to my day
nothing passing can now cease
I must diminish to increase
your growth shall buttress my decay
as continents are in the sea
your existence is in me

I ASK NO THANKS

I ask no thanks for making you
I cannot think you wholly good
of all the pride and shame I know
seeds are dormant in your blood

It is your birthright to exult
to you time's whisper is a roar
but I find living difficult
this is what you will blame me for

Failure you will blame me for
whether of the world or you
because I made you what you are
and knew the world I bore you to

But in your triumphs I shall have
no share because you will have built
out of the rudiments I gave
a daughter to annul my guilt

FOURTH CHILD

As you are my fourth child I know how to handle you
nothing can take from us the joy we now give each other
but I wonder into what kind of girl you will grow
and remember how harshly I misjudged my mother

What I cannot do for you with love I do from fear
spinning my straw into the gold of your future
scrawling across the flag of your character
your childhood as my indelible signature

TO MY CHILDREN

Others may pity me but you shall not be ashamed
how can I scorn the life which is all I have
I will not belittle the little that I have saved
by denying my childhood memories my love

How can I wish to undo the past which I am
though I beggared myself I would not become another
'the appalling Jewish experience' is my own
'the unknown victims' are my father and mother

Be proud of the beginning you have in me
be proud of how far I have wandered with this burden
I would value you less if I were not a refugee
your presence changes my wilderness to a garden

GERARD . M . KENNY

L♥VES

CHERYL . A . LLOYD

SOS 2=2 SOS

ALWAYS
AND
FOREVER

MONOLOGUES

I

Children are Windfalls

Children who might have been mine
from choice or by chance
wait till I am alone
to come out and prance
on my mind's stage
as if I were a barren peasant
beset with age

All children are windfalls
sometimes these others
are suddenly present
as sounds are in bells
in their sisters and brothers

II

Mothers Waiting

Mothers waiting for school to be out
are patient and content
but how much we resent
our children when we are faced with them

In anticipation proud
in reality we feel
a mixture of guilt for the dream
and shame at the facts they reveal

III

Stella's Eyes

My daughter grieves over inadequate eyes
they are an example of
love being not enough
nobody else can see what she can see

All appearances are a disguise
we all look at the world alone
she wears her body wrapped about
her vulnerability
so that it is as hard to look in
as it is for her to look out

IV

Stella's Imperfections

Perfection makes my daughter self-contained
when I admire her I make no claim
imperfections which we share
make me feel related to her
I discover them with love
and am ashamed
because however much I disapprove
I cannot wish her to be free of them

V

Christopher's Grief

Grief makes my growing children withdraw from
tentative outposts and turn back to me
sad that only life's hostility
can prolong my usefulness to them

A sudden need for being comforted
contradicts my son's age
briefly he has reverted to the stage
of having faith in me and being led

VI

Looking after Naomi

Why, when I do so much for her all day long,
do I resent some minor demand she makes?
This pressure on each moment till it breaks,
is it not spring?

When she pours her existence into the mould of my day,
what a vessel she fashions!
What value would I have left to lock away
if she did not count me among her possessions?

VII

Naomi Praised

I need to hear my children praised
they are the pyramids I build
and like a slave I only see
immediate concerns to me

Spectators view the total child
the shape revealed leaves me amazed

VIII

Stella's Hair

My daughter's hair has been styled to remind me of home:
one Friday night I prayed beside this head.
Whenever I look at my children I think there
are children whom the Germans would have killed.
My imagination has seen them starving and dead.

How can my daughter be protected from
such a weapon in the style of her hair?

IX

Encouraging Naomi

I encourage my youngest to think that she is important
I shall leave it to life to teach her humility
she looks English but was born a Jew
that she will suffer is certain

Though I can spare her nothing I can arm her
so that whatever happens cannot harm her
as much as what has happened has harmed me

X

I Teach my Children

I teach my children independence all the time
I taught them to walk till they ran out of the house
I taught them to speak and they have made other friends
I teach my daughters to copy my hands with their hands
until they can do the work no longer mine
all the time I teach my children to say yes
to the beginning where their need for me ends

TOUCH

(I)

A caress does more than appease
the hunger for touch:
practising the compassion of the flesh,
the body throws
– as music throws the dancer –
the mind into poses to please,
which mirror-poses answer.

(II)

An accidental contact makes no claim.
A caress is different because it communicates choice.
Behind the touch which we are used to lies
a reservoir of bankrupt piracy.
Like ants at warfare signals issue from
unchallengeable familiarity.

IN THE NEW LIBERAL SYNAGOGUE

I

How could Cain know what he had done the rabbi said
when he had never before seen this change
death came into the world with Abel dead

The listeners are exiled German Jews
sitting side by side each in his isolation
as a child I watched an angel choose
six million victims from this congregation
not to have died to have survived is strange

Let no one hesitate to mention to us
the killing of one human by another
the way to understanding passes through us

Cain did not know what he was doing to his brother

II

My neutral daughter is aware
that sheltered by my family
in God I am less close to her
than in the world's hostility

But can she see the mark we bear?

III

My daughter feels exempt and slightly bored
I have not taught her how to celebrate
now the traditions which I have ignored
challenge their echo in her to relate
her sturdy lifetime to the salvaged word

I think of children dying of starvation
six months I would have lived the records show
my feelings make a fence of all I know
between my daughter and this congregation

IV

I imagine my mother in any middle-aged woman
dressed in black warm and fat as she was when I was a
    child
my mind which can be compassionate to a German
has no pity for me and shows her about to be killed

The exiled choir sings its praise
in German Jewish melodies
we do not question God who made
men vulnerable and afraid
and others suffer more than us
nor in our father's house refuse
to rejoice that we are Jews

VI

Nothing this evening is for me what it seems
this synagogue is the symbol of another
my daughter is myself I am my mother
those around us have died in concentration camps
beyond this hall are other holy rooms
in which all the survivors worship together

AN EXAMINATION

The doctor demonstrated on my shins
that I was born into a time of famine
Germany nineteen twenty-three I said
not parentage but history determines
the substances from which our selves are made
beneath the jargon of my seven skins
my Jewish skeleton is branded German

ISRAEL NOTEBOOK 1966

I

Influenced by their own German childhood memories,
they told me not to burden my children with being Jews –
forgetting the wrecked lorries on the road to Jerusalem
commemorating the courage of those who died in them.

My half-Jewish children will grow up to make their
    choice.

In the *Yad Vashem* I heard an English child
asking: 'And he was going to be killed?'
intoning the statement like a ritual imposed
by every photograph of the Holocaust.

'And they were going to be killed?' still asks the voice.

II

Anyone coming upon this grave without warning
might think some warrior king lies buried there
and that the names are of the battles he fought.
Six million dead need space only in thought.
If they could become birds they would fly clear
of this rock roof which will not admit the morning.

III

The salmon sun on camel ground
hatches ghetto beards of scrub
this is a concept more than land
to raise who were defeated up

God's dereliction where he pottered man,
green orchestration of Messianic dreams,
are the south and north of both exile and home,
where every year of the expectation of life
is represented by another nation –
all people whom the Germans would have killed.

Ancient Jerusalem is ruin-grey –
the ash of history raked to a crown;
oriental Jewish children play
within the range of rifles pointed down.

From desert stone, in legendary places,
an ancestry of pride is being built
by survivors with contaminated faces –
all people whom the Germans would have killed.

That we come from the desert explains the Jew.
Where nothing obstructs the shadow of man
or intervenes between eye and horizon
what can be imagined may be true.

A tyranny of concepts grew
in this petrified sea of pink and gold
where the world is what a life can hold.
The desert we come from explains the Jew:

Stunted, conditioned victims who,
yielding essence like a fruit,
danced in the presses of pursuit –
that we come from the desert explains the Jew.

VII

This is the country of the resurrection:
its people carry dead relatives in their eyes,
tend them for harvest in ghettos of remembrance,
hoard them against hunger where children are evergreen.

Behind the victims pilloried to pity
are granaries of healthy generations;
the whole dispersion irrigates this triumph
where history grows fresh interpretations.

EXPLOSION

Today began days which began days ago
when some chose violence from all of life
broke daily bread domesticating death
and farmed destruction with the dung of hate

A bus full of children exploded in the desert
making a seismograph of every heart
setting alight a firework of fighters
the fuse of Auschwitz gaining on their birthright

Helicopters are flying over Jerusalem
tomorrow begins with the casualties of today
enmity is the closest relationship of all
more urgent than life, every death a regeneration

I SET OUT FOR JERUSALEM

I set out for Jerusalem,
leaving my father and my mother,
when I sloughed off my childhood skin.
Before, when I was coined a Jew
by all the mints of Germany,
I set out for Jerusalem.
Before that, when my grandfather
with legends and with candlelight
forged for me a shield of pride.
When my infant senses met
reality instead of home,
I set out for Jerusalem.

I belong with those who kept
a Jerusalem of thought
as a refuge from the world,
guardians of splinters which
constitute our heritage.
Two thousand years of wilderness
from which the caretaker has swept
the excrements of history
are kindled to a radiance
in which motes of people dance –
pollen out of dust, to be
sustenance for prophecies.

Need to belong has made me come
to help rebuild Jerusalem,
where everyone is family –
all descendent from Abraham
and sharing one inheritance.
Where every step is taken by

one entering my father's house,
and every stone is laden with
the honey of remembrances,
my right hand is relearning to
renew me with community –
closer for containing me.

NIGHTFALL IN JERUSALEM

Purple, the light flows over the pallid stones
surrendering the pollen of the sun.
The desert drives its goats across the sky.

Messianic rock with people in its veins,
that has been crouching since the world began,
rises, each grain a fountain to the eye.

THE CHILDREN IN THE STREET

None of the children here ever walk on their own:
the scenes around them hand them through the streets,
their senses buckled into the armour of home.
Life kneels to its reflection in their faces.
None of the children are ever still, in response
to the sap of the city rising in their spring.

ENCOUNTERS

The ground is singing under our feet:
who were cast aside like stones have sprung up as harvest,
life rekindled by community.
The past ploughed under whispers as we meet:
you are my neighbour whose roots nourish me.

NAOMI IN JERUSALEM

I

One generation past the holocaust
my golden daughter matches Jerusalem:
all she expends herself on contributes to make her.

II

People, noises and events
are my daughter's elements
and the honey-coloured stones
dance about her in response.

MY CHILDREN WALK IN JERUSALEM

A German girl came to my door,
saying she was the daughter of
someone I played with as a child.
I thought of how I was allowed
to use Margaret's garden swing:
that such a thing was event enough
forty years later to be recalled
implies the weight of the chains I wore.
I have lived with my memories for so long,
by now the poison has drained out.

My children walk in Jerusalem
engaged in life and unconcerned
that history makes use of them
to balance old iniquities.
They have no ghetto memories:

English country children who
belong to the Messianic age,
when the German sits down with the Jew
whom nothing now distinguishes
because his people has returned.

My children walk in Jerusalem
among the resurrected Jews
stronger collectively through them:
like jewels the crowd wears their eyes,
and future days bow down like sheaves.
All the graves of Europe have
closed before my children's gaze,
all the survivors have come through
a wilderness of grief to see
this Phoenix generation grow.

ON THE TERRACE

As sun reflected sometimes dazzles sight –
suddenly, in the midst of conversation
as I was sitting among friends at night
Jerusalem outlined in lights below –
my mind was dazzled by the thought of you
and I was glad, not out of calculation
because of what might come to me through you
but glad that you exist and that I know

NOTES TO CAROL

(for my grandson)

I

Babyhood to be complete
needs grandparents at head and feet;
six make a fence of family.
Michael's has been broken as
that of Michael's father was
by the hounds of history.

II

There is no such thing as the evil eye
and anyone may look at him;
but those who look at him don't see
the stopped earth of the fox of time.

III

Babies do not start from scratch.
Michael's caul told that I am
alien where he is at home:
before he grew his sense of sight
he crouched behind my eyes to watch
England receive me as a child.

IV

On a green island Michael grows
where villages bear legendary names
and moody seas dispute the rocky shore.
Before he learns to listen he will hear
the desert sighing in the summer rain.

MY TWO DAUGHTERS

I

My two daughters are the one fair, the one darker;
the colour of their hair is their badge of character.

II

The older one, my winter daughter, has
the quality of water under ice.
Like peasants from a lake, I draw
sustenance through the ice I thaw.

III

Stella harbours out of sight,
as bulbs do flowers, seeds of light;
she brings them out like ornaments.
Questing beast and quarry pause
to gaze through her forest eyes
at her firework of plants.

IV

Extracting colours out of mood
and patterns out of solitude,
Stella, like a sorceress,
compels adversities to bless.
An eagle urge beneath the skin
unpicks stars and thorns the shroud
of girlhood she is captive in.

V

As a well is to a fountain, Stella is to her sister,
who has no patience with passivity,
milks to exhilaration each fat day –
a Goldilocks who does not run away.

VI

All the adversities that attended her birth
were routed by a whisper of her worth.
Death left its hoof-mark on her scalp to turn
into good what comes to do her harm.

VII

Naomi, made to be
my ransom to history,
has fallen, to succour me,
far from her parent tree.
All of existence thrives
because she is alive.

VIII

My dandelion daughter moves
where faces turn as if to light,
I wish that she may always find
herself more loving than being loved,
and that what she seems at sight
does not belie the girl within.

STELLA GOING

I

My daughter has been leaving me all the time.
From the moment of birth I have been letting her go.
You cannot own daughters and all daughters grow
out of their father, their mother and their home.

Who am I to be discontent after seventeen years
that she is leaving me – can you call it alone,
when so much of me has turned Stella that I can
make her accept so much of myself as hers?

While life has been adding to Stella and Stella to me,
she has been going away from me all the time,
transferring to independence crumb by crumb
the mortar joining us as family.

II

Mothers are made out of the daughters they were.
I am pig-in-the-middle to my mother and Stella,
as if I were my mother and as if Stella were me.
I am the catalyst which those two share.

Stella is going from me as I went from my mother.
Continuity has blown its fuse in me,
imposing what was on what is going to be.
I am brand-marked 'mothers and daughters don't stay
    together'.

At every moment I remember how
I broke impatiently from the final embrace:
because of my failure as a daughter I face
what it meant for my mother to be my mother, now.

III

All conversations with
which I have tried to build
our relationship –
being mother and child –
into one holding good
throughout your adulthood
have been sabotaged by
my lack of experience of
being an adult daughter:
knowing my mother after
rejecting her where she stood,
which your going from me
now is a variant of.

IV

Don't look back at the anxious small woman who stands
with the reins you have slipped in her middle-aged hands,
she will cause you to stumble with a grey glance.
She will cast her blood as a river before you,
eject her womb as a wolf to devour you,
and dress her bones in your skin to dance.

Make for the gap in the hedge of horizon,
your parental pasture's become a prison –
time to begin your original fable.
Don't look back for the face behind the curtain,
it's the future about which you have to be certain.
Prove of what you're capable.

My Daughters, My Sisters

TONY

My younger son has tried to die:
swallowing sleeping pills to scrap
twenty-one years of growing up.
It makes no sense though he wrote why.

My gay and golden comforter
has come in from the world to lay
a stranger bearded beyond play
across the saddle of my care.

II

Tony is lying unconscious in hospital,
his dream of dying vomit in his mouth.
Doctors and nurses resurrect him with
first aid as if his hurt were physical.

III

Like honeysuckle Tony clung
when he was little and I was young.

He was fat and primed with life
when he got his first pocket knife,
trusted the arms of the sea
before he grew too big for mine
and learned to handle rod and line
before he knew his ABC.
He had a loyal passion for
toys that rose into the air.
He went through boyhood gathering
the cuckoo-spit of mothering.

81

Tony put his feet up on the world's table,
believing it his birthright to be happy,
and round him grew a hedge of friends
sheltering him from life's demands.

V

Moony Tony longed to be
like a firework at night.
Moony Tony set alight
the gunpowder of reality.

TONY GONE

I

My children's doings are their lives not mine:
to me they are weather from over the hill of age.
Tony has gone with his fistful of wants like tickets
to plague some gatekeeper to let him in.
I listened to the whistling in the thicket
and did not think of the neglected cage.

II

I can think of Tony as if he were a stranger:
it is years ago since I felt the bond of flesh.
We reject adolescent children to set them free.
I believed that he no longer needed me
so long before he needed me no longer
that he is like an underfired pot.

I constantly think of life letting go and smash
this stranger to me – and know that he is not.

TONY ALONE

a.

Tony feels lonely when he is alone,
he needs other people as colour needs light,
knowing that all is relative
and the world outnumbers him one to one.

b.

He thinks that he is only Tony:
a button on the coat of life,
and that it does not matter if
he rolls off into the gutter.

c.

Cold in the prison of his skin
he wraps himself in company;
it does not cure the boy within:
laying a girl does not make a man.

II

Tony belongs to his generation,
he wears the uniform of its knights
in quest of the twentieth century grail;
nothing he learned as a child has taught him
how to spring the traps on this trail.
Growing mature is a sort of migration:

finding out who he is has brought him
– Tony smashed reassembling the bits –
to look at himself by the light of strangers,
threshing experience green on the stalk,
community yielding him all that he hungers for,
each gift a hammer blow leaving its mark.

TONY IN CLOVER

I

Having outgrown his father and his mother,
Tony's exchanged one pasture for another.

I, who am still defenceless against his demands,
know someone will always give him what he wants.

Now he has gone the unclaimed supplies for his needs
are choking the threshold of my days like weeds.

II

My mind has stored up
all of his babyhood:
never will he depend
on any other woman
as he did on me, completely;
he may love her as sweetly:
she'll not be in his blood;
though now we're out of step
and he thinks a beginning
what I think of as an end.

A DOUBLE WEDDING

I

Throughout their boyhood they made a track,
spilling me like sawdust from a sack.

Now strangers have flooded the workings where
together we mined their characters.

Time swallows me up while they try to escape
from the hollow within them still holding my shape.

II

Beyond what I mean to them,
they don't know who I am.

They look at me with surprise
– strangers – through their brides' eyes.

They've half destroyed me to pull
their sturdy roots up whole.

III

As a diverted stream
changes character,
so I am altered by
being channelled through
this increased family
where the old must look to the new.

MY SONS' BRIDES

When they came like princesses
demanding my sons,
I gave up the garments
and kept the bones.

They have taken their captives
to grind them to bread,
who might have been harnessed
to the world instead.

At the height of their power
they shall learn mercy
and break into flower
incarnating me.

GENERATIONS

The Male Line

I

Like caterpillars
my two sons
ate the leaves of my girlhood
till they were gone.

Faithful to the legend
of the primeval curse
they killed each other
for seventeen years.

Like berries in hedges
lies the fat time
they have gone to harvest
away from home.

II

My father was a fortress,
my sons are stone,
I am the river
flowing between.

The fortress is a ruin,
my sons have grown tall,
I am the descent of
the waterfall.

My sons are stepping-stones
in the water:
I have surfaced a mother
where I drowned a daughter.

III

They have inherited through me
the pogrom-eaten ghetto roots
of Central European Jews
who gave themselves to Germany,
and tribal memories of rites
against divine indifference,
old vulnerabilities,
and archetypes that influence
who they are and what they do.

87

IV

My grandson, like the almond tree,
blossoms in inclement weather.
With a runaway for a father
(without the parents of his father)
what shall he do for family?

Michael, milk the circumstances,
a tree grows stronger for standing alone.
With no footsteps to follow, pioneer.
The dyes of generations·are
stored in the roots of your seedling senses:
proof that you are not on your own.

V

My father gave Tony
behind the back of time
the reins of his boyhood
for me to hunt him down.

Throughout the orchestration
of Tony's puppy days
my father called 'cuckoo'
from before I was.

Bread for an orphan
Tony gave to me
when he caught up my father
and I looked through his eyes.

My grandfather used ritual
to comfort his mortality.
The first time I gave birth I thought
if all the life I burned were caught
within the fruit rehousing me
that would make satisfaction whole.
But he roused such a sense of guilt
through proving me inadequate
it made me turn towards the dead
as all the family I had.

MY FATHER'S HOUSE

I

I was more like a wayside plant,
when I grew in my sisters' shade,
than one a gardener would praise:
from them I drew my nourishment.
The one was magpie-sharp and proud,
the other dark and diffident,
and I as youngest was allowed
by them an insect's liberties.

II

Eager in my Eden
to catch my sisters up,
I hurried through my childhood
till it made my mother weep.

I entered the trinity
chastised and purged:
Anne was hammer, Lisa anvil
when I was forged.

III

I called her second sister who
in childhood always put me first,
she was the shadow side of me,
where all that was not good enough
for my eldest sister grew.
I could not have deserved her much.
And only now I realise
that there was a relationship
which by-passed me between those two.
Though Anne has been dead for thirty years
and only my second sister and I
have survived our father's house,
it wounds me to think that perhaps
they loved each other more than me.

IV

My mother had three daughters,
the first was her crown,
the second her ransom,
and I her chains.

When I was the captain
with the dew on my heart,
my sisters the pirates
drove us into port.

When I ran from my mother
before I could stand,
my enemy sisters
took me by the hand.

With one besieged mother
between us three,
they hunched their shoulders
and hoisted me.

V

The first girl whom my mother bore
and put into my father's hands
made him feel ignorant and strong,
for even Anne was malleable
until she had learned being Anne.
He did not hold her fast for long.
After a year he turned to one
less challenging in her demands,
who had inherited his eyes
and taught him fatherhood before
I made her give him up to me
(by then he would have liked a son)
who did not care whether he was
sensitive, infallible
or, as my mother wanted, kind,
but only asked him to impose
– to brand-mark me as family –
his maker's imprint on my mind.

VI

I see him as a stately man
being pursued by three small girls
in rivalry for his two hands;
whenever he turns they become
dolls making no demands on him,
scared of a camaraderie
that captured enemies as friends
but did not know how to address
a daughter craving a caress.
I still wish he would wait for me
who in imagination hurl
myself over the brink of time:

not for the sake of snatching what
I have balanced life without,
but to let me take one step
in step with him to mitigate
that lonely progress eating up
the road he trusted where it ends.

MY DAUGHTERS, MY SISTERS

I

Remembering children, I confuse
my daughters' childhood with my own.
As they grow older I become,
the more I think of them as home,
the little sister who must choose
to follow them or be left alone.

II

There are five of us in the childhood yard.
That we are related shows in our faces.
Now I am the age our mother was
when we went from her, my sisters become
my daughters when I look back at them.
I can love them better now because
my daughters have taught me how to give.
By mirroring some of their traits they have
brought them again within my reach.
My daughters, my sisters, have changed places:
as I stood as a child I stand as a mother,
seeing the others turn towards each other,
tolerating me, on their guard
against one who is demanding too much.

I have borne daughters to inherit Anne
off whom I fed with all my senses,
they are the lanterns she shines through.
She is the prompter whom they copy when
the imperfections I passed on to them
make them take thought as they recite their lives.
They have left me standing to hurry after,
one earnestly and the other laughing,
Anne in oblivion juggling chances
challenging them to be her crew.
They have picked like apples what was worth having
from where they nested while they were small;
with me it is autumn now they are leaving me,
time makes me humble which makes them tall.
Anne in death remains their generation,
(it is me they copy, running to the source)
she will share with them, who are her inventions,
all the years which she did not use.

COMPARED WITH SINGLE WOMEN . . .

Compared with single women
I am something of a slave;
even at night, when I wake
while my sons and daughters are dreaming,
I am like one who must take
her pitcher to the well:
it's then that I remake
all my world until
it's the kingdom I think I deserve.
With only herself to serve,
who would not choose to lie still?

CONTACT

Touch, like a threat, makes me adapt
to what each of my children demands;
they light me up till the contact breaks
and I revert, inviolate,
to my dark state.

But beyond the gate of the senses,
my sons and daughters have grown
not within fences, like plants,
but – mingling with me –
like waters joining the sea.

SOMETIMES MY MOTHER . . .

Sometimes my mother shines
out of Naomi's face,
making her hers more than mine,
taking her out of my reach,
and my emotions race
back to my childhood to pay
the debt of love which I owe her
and fetch my daughter away.

ANTI-LOVE SONG

for Naomi

Don't love me constantly,
and not so much:
leave me free sometimes,
when I feel at odds
with the world and myself,
to reject your touch,

and to hate you a little
in certain moods
that you give me cause only
for self-reproach.

IN THE MUSEUM

for Stella

The size of the portal and
the durableness of stone
make her appear small and frail
as she passes through to stand –
in the brightness of the hall
momentarily apart
like a rejected sparrow –
before some work of art,
while images run wild
on the canvas of her mind;
maybe Michelangelo
stood like that as a child.

TO STELLA GROWING UP

When all of you was part of me,
what part of you broke through to be
free and grow independently,
the first leaf of Stella? And how much
of me was carried into the bud?
Are you aware of my presence there
– like blight, of darkness and of light –
as you get to know your identity?
Will you let it stay or bid it go?

TOUCHING STELLA

As she grows I let go.
But my touch remains on her skin:
by it she measures how much
others who reach for her mean to her
beyond the appeal of the flesh,
because when she started living
she could not distinguish between
the giving of love and its feel.

STELLA GONE

I

Absence is a sort of death:
I have to think you alive,
challenging the dimensions with
tenacity and love.

I filled a thought of you with breath
until it had your shape –
were you aware of it when the teeth
of time took you by the nape?

II

The distance between us is winter,
it blackens the buds of thought:
the more I allow you to matter,
the more I must do without.

You have become my snowgirl,
to be cherished with restraint.
All the spoils of self-conquest
remain ours to spend.

STELLA REMEMBERED

Stella remembered doesn't move,
as if my mind, storing up sight,
made of it something like pressed flowers.

I used to look at her day and night
when she was a baby, not to lose
anything through the sieve of hours.

Now I am ready to barter years
of photographs for a memory
showing her turning towards me.

IN THE ABSENCE OF STELLA

Why should I miss you
when others are with me
and I wear their touch
on my skin like a badge:
I have children enough.
In the absence of you
they're merely jetsam;
they only compete
when you're at home
and I'm complete.

AFTER A QUARTER OF A CENTURY

My nature, that of a slave
who wants to serve and please,
is not rewarded by
my children setting me free;
I thought of getting away
when they overgrew me like weeds,
their needs leaving no space for mine –
and stayed in my place
because I found that I am
standing up by supporting them.

FOSTER-ENGLAND

The Land

Feeling closer to
the long-dead savages
from whose traces grow
ancestral images
than to the living men
with their 'how-do-you-do'
who lock their faces
against one like me,
I wish that I had come
in that century
when the mingling of races
made this their home.

The Language

Silent in Babylon
my sad fathers
laid my inheritance
on the flowing waters,
like the seed in the flesh,
word within anguish,
to grant me speech
in an alien language.

The Boy

A London boy caught
in his grey estate
skating down thoughts
to reach escape
with all green England
for his wage
and the cold sea tempered
in his look
and a swagger in
his Viking hair
took me to share
his anchorage.

MARRIED LOVE

I

One never feels as grown-up as one looks.
Mothers need fathers when their children do.
The first time our first child cried and you
picked him up and held him in your hands
I was like a girl with a doll in front of a stranger.
That was the moment I stopped being orphaned:
not when you married me but when you took
a share in my responsibilities.
You looked a giant and he looked a dwarf,
he looked as if he had come out for the hour,
the most vulnerable part of me
exposed screaming to reality
taking possession of your fatherhood.

II

We judge by what we feel and others do.
I was a tight-rope walker when we met.
You did not act as if you were one too:
balanced convincingly on a pinpoint of pride.
It made me confident to walk with you
holding my hand as if you knew the way
because you were at home where I was not.
I remember you leaning on an autumn fence,
part colour of the English countryside –
and all the distance between us being downhill,
I ran like a river from my inheritance
to join you rejoicing and make you my guide
where all the cross-roads left no choice at all.

III

To turn a stranger into family
takes more self-confidence than I possessed
when we were young. You did not hurry me.
Knowing that all life is impermanent,
I sought a home it would not hurt to lose
which would outweigh for me the one I lost.
Now that you have been closest to me longer
than anyone else, much longer than my parents
(and all the time I have been renewed and changed)
you lie green in the membranes of my senses
and rise like sap in my experiences.
If we met by chance and if we were free to choose,
I was less incomplete without you younger.

LATE SUMMER

I

None except you knows that in my fiftieth year
I can be unsettled, like a girl, by a look;
I keep my balance unless you are near me,
stirring me into life enough to show
what is lying in wait for me: don't go.
Don't go.

II

I love especially your body's imperfections,
which signal to mine that desire is tougher than youth:
all the years I have lived pour into the joy of touch;
though the senses grow blunter, sensation grows more acute
as we struggle together against each other's rejection.

I constantly question whether I have known
the ecstasy of flesh of which some speak;
perhaps they're boasting, or perhaps they mean
the feeler coming out of every cell
piercing the shell in which we live alone.

IV

Look at the women of my generation:
who except former lovers will love them now
to keep them malleable in compensation
for all they abdicate, that they may grow
older opening out, as children do.

LOVE POEM

I

All who have loved me,
blood-relations and you,
knowing better than I
who I ought to be,
amateur gods all,
once thought me good:
as tough as a weed,
like a chord to the touch,
the jug for survival —
till I blundered like Eve,
demanding too much.

II

I match my love to my beloved.
I don't know what pours me so full
that I must be tapped or overflow:
then I call like a bell and favour all
and give myself and am still whole
and hold on tight even to one
who looks down the well and throws a stone
to know by the echo how deep I go.

III

Matching my love to my beloved,
who was my mother on a beach
when others were beyond my reach
and only she surrounded me,
I lay like one of her own limbs
in the bay of her lap lapped by her breath –
in the net of the sun skin against skin
till her flesh reopened to let me in –
when she woke to a summons beyond my range,
broke me off and stopped being mine.

IV

Delight in touch
is part of love;
I've handled my children's
bodies so much
when they were little,
one would think it enough;
they come back as grown-ups
and use their stings
on my hands and lips
to draw mothering.

V

When I was a daughter my father stood
like Samson holding my childhood up;
communicating no more than God,
caught in this flash of his lightning blood
like the chance of light in a drop of water:
I sought out his weakness to trap his love
riding in coverts beyond my horizon,
not realising that I must be
– matching my love to my beloved –
diminished by my victory.

In whom I love
I am at home;
my parents, my sisters,
I have outgrown,
my sons, my daughters,
are outgrowing me,
and who remains
except you, except you?

TOUCH

To court me with your touch,
be ceremonial;
it's what distinguishes
contact by choice of love
from that of family,
with whom it's orchestration,
not the theme as between us:
it's the physical response
by which we measure how much
our relationship means.

SEPARATION

Children playing at statues
till they're released by touch
exploit a primary truth:
contact keeps the flesh warm.
Your absence spreads a chill
from which no spell can guard me;
myself on my mother's arm,
our babies on mine –
such memories reward me
with a calm which will turn me to stone.
To remain flesh I must burn.

COMPULSION

The first boy who kissed me
had your sort of hair;
like you, my father
– also a peaceful man –
when young looked a soldier;
all my feelings have fed
on the giblets of my story:
I reject you as I did
my mother before you
round whom I still am
like flesh on the bone.

TOUCHING FLESH

She, who would not let me
– loving her so much –
ever even touch her,
when lying dead
was taken possession of by
the inanimate things about her:
shrinking as it cooled, her flesh
could not be cherished without her.
I, seeing her body – all that
was left of Anne – betray her,
wanted to touch it but
continued to obey her.

DEATH IN CLAPTON

Woman Dying

The sheet worn fine with use
against the coarsening skin
does not conceal the eyes
still letting the light in;
nothing else moves as she lies.
The dark familiar room
draws dark brown shadows from
the pattern of the bones
about the china blue eyes.
They poise themselves to rise
beyond pain and be free,
beyond fear, till they see
and close their sight upon
the dying woman, alone.

The Photograph

No one who knew her then
remains alive to recall
her zest for living when
all must have seemed possible,
with her proud youth to give,
serenely confident
that such as she would have
what promised her content;
before the grit of the years
blunted the blade of her will
and she submitted to cares
and the strength of her senses went
into keeping her passions still.

The House

Sounds sent years ago
up the spine of the stairs
now douse with dusty echoes
others climbing there.

Dark wardrobes are weeping
over beds and chairs
soft, colourful clothes
the dead are keeping.

A disused curtain stirs:
fresh air blows through a crack.
The mirror shows a photograph
of one who will not be back.

AT A RECEPTION

Now I am glad to be one whom people ignore:
none except we know that you have singled me out.
Shaking hands as if you had not kissed my eyes,
exchanging memories of touch, let go before
others can see you making me become
the most exciting woman in the room.

THROUGH MY HANDS

After all the uses
to which I have put my hands,
it is miraculous
that touching you they can
record a new response;
although they settle on
impervious surfaces
which cannot capture them,
they give me access past
the sentries of the flesh
to reach the man within
who holds me fast.

UPHOLD ME

And still my feelings sprout richest
in the furrow ploughed by my father:
caress me as a daughter
to gather a total harvest.
I accept you with every blemish,
as I did the man in my childhood,

as a measure of my own value;
be David to make me Bathsheba,
elaborate me with legends,
uphold me in the image
I formed of myself when I was
indomitable like grass
and passion lay fallow

LOVE SONG

Love me familiarly,
without humility,
as Adam did Eve who had
once been a part of him;
shine on me directly
so that no chink of doubt
can take your warmth from me;
don't let me fail to be
the instrument you think:
be masterful, make me
respond in harmony.

GOODNIGHT TO NAOMI

Why is putting my cheek against yours an expression of love?
'm as hungry for contact with you as if it could heal me,
could turn time away while you remain little enough
with a baby's reaction to my skin in your cheeks)
o need me so much that you have the need to feel me.

FAMILY SUM

I turn now to one of my children, now to another,
who wanting their mother must all turn to me:
if each of the four should need me one quarter as much
as I need them, a sort of balance is struck,
which satisfies me till I question whether
I give out four times as much as I get back.

BY NOW MY FATHER . . .

By now my father would be an old man.
I look at old men to see myself in their eyes.
I hold your hand in which the years are humming
notes of the tune with which my life began
to feel the death in which my father lies.

WORDS

With no talent for living, I often wish myself dead;
my single asset is a sense of words:
for their sake I accept myself as I am.
At times I have ringed and released them singing like birds
to find another mind elsewhere that made
a cage for them in which they felt at home.

Coming Back from Babylon

SARAH

I

A desert nomad was
Sarah, my ancestress,
and her home must have been
a tent like the Bedouin's.

Oh let me be among,
she must have prayed when young,
the women who bear sons.

Since they feared kings would kill
the Patriarch for her sake
she must have been beautiful.

Her sterile beauty made the desert dance.

II

She walked the desert with the world at stake,
all offspring, small blind creatures made her weep,
oh why, she wept, am I not like the others –
the cry is part of my inheritance,
asking for mercy not for miracles,
all children are born to the death of mothers.

Weeping she walked the desert of God's sleep
and knew his phantasies about the Jews,
Isaac dying through the centuries,
and thinking of his children wept for me,
and with her pity kept his birth at bay.

III

The desert which remade in stone
the pits and pillars of the sun
made God from what it knew of men.

In a camel-coloured tent
Sarah laughed and clapped her hands.

IV

Old age fell from her like the peel of fruit;
a mirage baby skipped across the sands.
Be mine, she called, I'll mother all mankind,
allow me love and I'll be satisfied.
Feeling his fragile skull against her throat
weighted with Auschwitz and Christ crucified
she called, I'm willing! to the desert wind.

JEPHTHAH'S DAUGHTER

I

Knowing her future she went to the hills,
one might have thought it was to meet a lover;
the leaves, the insects whispered to each other,
to die so young and be so excellent!
If it was spring she would not see it ending
and flowers hastened to be where she went.

She stands for my dead sister, for my youth,
for all the sacrifices life demands –
this girl in Gilead who redeemed her father
with frailty more invincible than arms.

Since die we must it is a grace
to see the world not slacken pace;
wild things about her called, escape!
At night a lion kept her warm.
She did not argue with her fate,
the nameless girl with my sister's face,
lest someone had to take her place.

III

If she was like myself she made a song.
Oh land, she sang, of orange-groves and palms,
I would have planted vineyards in your deserts
and satisfied Jerusalem with psalms.
And all the birds of Israel about her
agreed to go on singing it without her.

And thoughts of all who died for being Jews,
in wars and at the stake and in the ghettos,
fell out of chaos and became the dew.

IV

While the almond-trees flowered
and the Jordan flowed on
she was like my sister
young and alone.

V

Oh world I love you, she sang to the land,
compared with life, what is a little dying?
In spirit she was like my sister strong.
Be one with me, she heard the land replying;
and still in Gilead when the sap is rising
the hills do homage to her with their spring.

SAMSON IN GAZA

I

They mocked him after he became a slave,
the citizens of Gaza flocked to see him:
the blinded giant with a convict's pate –
for twenty years the Judge in Israel;
they brought their skinny children to feel brave
as they threw stones at Samson in his chains.

Thus Nazi Germany was entertained.

II

He thought, they have my body,
they shall not have my mind,
I will not curse humanity
because of the Philistines;
and he comforted his body
with thoughts of Jerusalem.

III

The sweetest pots we women bake
in the bliss of our wombs
men fill with pride and anger
and sport with till they're ruined.

IV

Such grappling-irons must have come
out of the furnace of his eyes
his captors could not suffer them.

V

One on whose body he had strummed his tune
stood constantly among the changing crowd;

he felt her look and thought it was the sun.
God was no friend, she sighed, when he made man,
we should have been less cruel or less frail.
Long after he was dead, when she was old,
he was still whole and virile in her mind;
but she had loved him better for his wounds.

VI

My father too was made a slave –
God spoils good tools to mend the world;
mourn every hero as a man.
To himself Samson wasn't brave,
I see him with my father's face;
the hands that brought the pillars down
were gentle with his family,
and to one like myself he said,
comfort me.

RUTH

I

Who was that foreign girl who came
destitute to Bethlehem
to be one of Christ's ancestors?

She preferred exile to being alone.

When she stood in the market-square,
in her foreign clothes, of another race,
and was at once surrounded by
her dead husband's family
who knew her by her unknown face –
did she feel, I have come home?

II

She was a stranger even in her sleep:
did not share the language of their dreams;
perhaps one night she tried to run away
– none would have stopped her had she left by daylight –
through dusty alleys to the desert hills,
and saw the sun come up out of her birthplace
and thought it was a sign and felt afraid.
Let me belong, she whispered to the village,
I have come out of death to be remade,
and as the shadows shifted from the valleys
she saw the land as lovely and was glad.

III

I too have chosen to belong
where people see me as a stranger;
I think of Ruth in Bethlehem:
in the childhood of man, was it easier
– before Auschwitz and the crucifixion –
to undo the bonds of race
or did she also feel closer to
past and future generations
than to the people she lived among?

IV

She was a stranger even as a mother:
knew other lullabies and other games;
watching her son at alien rituals
– withholding half of his inheritance
for his sake or because she was ashamed –
she thought, where he belongs I am at home,
and whispered through the prayers of the others,
Oh Bethlehem, my comforter of stone,
oh honey in the desert that is man,
I love you better than I do my own.

ESTHER

I

All the girls wanted to play the queen:
Haman was Hitler when I was young;
but imagine the upstart orphan
in the marvellous palace of Shushan
daring to seek out the king.

II

I'm not alone, she thought, walking alone,
the corridors like harp-strings to her feet,
all those whose lives are threatened are with me,
and saw the mirrors multiply pogroms.

Oh God who raised me put me down, she prayed,
make me suffer but don't make me speak,
you've all mankind and I have only me;
and saw events fall out of memory
– the Jews enslaved, Jerusalem destroyed –
and found an ally in the words to say.

III

Like me, when she was a child
and was hungry and was cold
and the world about her lay
alien with hostility,
she must have heard her elders pray,
return us to Jerusalem,
and seen through green and dancing hills
the dawning of the citadel.

IV

Dressed as the queen and still a frightened child,
God's gamble on compassion between men
– I pity God, she thought, for needing me –
she grew like fire as she hurried on,
her people's fate like brambles to her feet.

Oh choose me wisely for their sake, she prayed,
seeing the millions slaughtered through the ages,
and make me equal to the world you made;
a girl you would have passed by in the street,
who squared her shoulders as she hurried on,
all future acts of courage in her wake.

MOSES' MOTHER

I

Be secret river, the woman sang,
surrendering her first-born child,
and shallow like the heart of man.

She was a slave in ancient Egypt and
it's possible that she was reconciled.
I think she knelt all night long on the bank
and begged and raged and thought of suicide
and cursed God at the coming of the dawn.

II

It happened elsewhere and in other times:
the birth of saviours costs whole generations
– all those expendable babies! – mourned
by mothers who cared nothing for salvation.

III

Small light of life, the mother sang,
my fragile son so finely made,
I am no shelter against fate,
I cast you out because I must;
and still she held him in her arms,
kissed him to feel that he was warm
and once more put him to her breast.

IV

Mankind is like a comet with a tail
of ruined mothers with accusing eyes,
(mine, too, saved me by our separation)
miracle-makers for a little while
when all we know of life is love for us.

V

Replete with a grief so small it cast
    no blemish on the sun,
she held life fast while life itself
    remained indifferent;
God tramples out the stars, she sang,
we are too insignificant,
it's men who do the harvesting of men.

VI

Perhaps the son dreamed of the slip of land
that would enslave mankind's imagination
– oases sprang up where his dream touched sand –
but to the mother it was martyrdom
to let his casket rock out of her hand.

DAVID AND ABISHAG

I

Were there lamps as they lay together,
the village girl and the old king,
after the servants had left?
Wiping her tears like a lover
with his warrior's fist,
he forgot that there had been others
more completely possessed.
They're tears of life, she whispered,
I saw you when you were young.

II

The father of our people, she thought,
    is only an old man,
I'd rather look for a peasant boy
    than stay here as a queen;
but it was the young King David
    she lay with in her dream.

III

In the eyes of the old man
crouched the beauty they had known;
all the bodies they had touched
were bloom on his fingertips;
as the earth has precious mines
he was jubilant within.

IV

I envy God for having thought of you
and life for having loved you for so long
and our land because it is your home

and our people who have served your fame,
the girl's thoughts started singing with the dawn,
I envy our dead who fought for you
and all your enemies who made you strong
and generations harvesting your name.

NOAH ON ARARAT

I

He must have met with silence and horizon:
colours of sky and earth and shades of green
– green fire comforting the chastened earth
nowhere higher than mere days of growth;
nothing stirred between him and the tide.

Where are the birds? he thought into the silence;
he thought, I am like Adam the first man.
The last, the vegetation answered him.

And only then he visualised the violence,
the corpses putrefying in the water,
the earthworm suffocating in the mud.

II

His only weapon was a little scream
lost in the screaming of the lost creation,
God I don't want to have survived, he screamed,
to be alone, to be your memory,
to provide you with other generations,
my sons to kill and to be killed in war;
they were not perfect, oh my friends and neighbours,
but they were not as evil as your slaughter.

III

The earth lay abject in its wealth before
the population streaming from the ark
and everything with wings at once took flight,
mopping the final moisture from the air
until both land and sky were flower-bright;
to live, to live, what breathed sang to the hour,
with life as unremembered as the light.

IV

A shabby leader ageing in the sun,
the babies of the ark about his feet
– God's hostages, he thought, who succoured me –
he looked at life and saw that it was young,
was bloody because it was newly born,
a bit of chaos troubled into form –
and followed when the others urged him on.

TOWARDS BABYLON

I

And did they not sing songs of home
trudging towards Babylon?
A population on the move,
almost the whole of Jerusalem:
any column of refugees
must resemble those exiled Jews
– treasure-trove among the nations –
mourning what they would not lose,
burdened with survival and
all they carried and left behind,
every life threshed out to be
another grain of history.

The hill was worn from where they caught
a last sight of Jerusalem;
the name would have meant nothing if
the world had not taught Jews to mourn.

III

Imagine them filling the landscape at night:
camp-fires sparking in the desert wind,
the lamentations where someone had died,
and somewhere children's voices raised in song
rejuvenating their inheritance;
I too sat singing there when I was young.

Perhaps some of the Babylonian guards,
sick of the messy after-pains of war
– long absence honeying their families –
sought out the orphans to be sold as slaves
and told them, you will be like our own,
offering homes instead of memories;
and all those persecuted through the ages,
still buds in Eden, shouted out, belong!
The children could not hear them for the song.

THE SACRIFICE OF ISAAC

I

A man who could not tolerate his sons,
the first cast out, he took the other one
to give him like a pagan to his God
(as God gave Christ, having cast out the Jews);
he strode before the boy he hardly knew
– a patriarch who had befriended kings –
as if to do an ordinary thing.

II

And Sarah watched them out of sight
as the womb gives up green bones;
the morning kept the chill of night
the dew stayed on the stones,
and in the desert of the day
the shadows did not go away.

III

Plump with growth were the limbs of the victim,
like a lizard's tongue were his eyes,
he still had on him the bloom of creation
– dry was the wood for the sacrifice.

IV

The hills arose to jubilate
when God declared Jerusalem
and vegetation sprang like deer
from Eden to bejewel them
– and slunk to make the jungle when
it heard what it would witness there.

V

They carry their stakes and they dig their graves
and they die defending merely their lives:
the only river Jerusalem has
is the flow of Jews who are sacrificed.
Oh kill me and save the ram for Christ,
the boy called out as he looked down the ages,
seeing his kinsman nailed to the cross
the centuries streaming from his side,
and fought his father when he unbound him
who thought that it was for the ram he cried.

OUT OF EDEN

I

Once out of Eden they began to age:
change God created when he punished man
and thought up death to be alone again
and then thought it absurd to waste the world
and, dreaming elsewhere, to be done with him,
let man be god enough to create man.

II

Eve pregnant went about the world
in search of creatures giving birth,
not knowing it she mothered them;
and every baby was the first.

III

Mary was not as alone
as Eve was giving birth to Cain;
gazelles and tigers did not come
to the crib in Bethlehem;
gentle both were and ignorant
of their sons' significance
and the love they had for them was the same.

IV

When she had daughters Eve discovered song.
Sweet replicas of me, she sang, be strong,
you are too vulnerable for too long!
not knowing what it was like to be young.

V

Imagine children playing where
primeval forest was before;
the sun shone faster for their sake;
and animals in Paradise
stood by the fence like prisoners
God looking through their eyes.

VI

All Eden heard Eve singing at her chores.
God blessed me with his punishment, she sang,
and gave a purpose to me who had none!
and felt absolved and pitied her no more.

COMING BACK FROM BABYLON

I

When they came back from Babylon
– children of the captivity,
Jerusalem standing in their hearts –
and saw the burned and broken stones
– foxes in the sanctuary –
and under beams and cooking pots
clothing around skeletons,
they stroked the desert dust aside
and as if praying said, we're home.

II

The elders mourned, remembering
   Jerusalem despoiled,
but the young laughed at their labour
saying, bless old Pharaoh
   who taught us to build.

At night we walked about the ruined city
– the starlight set out before we were born;
following my parents' memories
I found the house – but every house was home.
And suddenly the stones stood up again
– there were people everywhere – we were besieged –
I smelled the burning and I heard the cries
and saw the casualties and felt the pain.

IV

Let others build their lives, they said,
    we build Jerusalem;
to outlast our enemies
    we build with more than stone.
One drop of blood all Jews gave up:
    they did not build alone.

LOT'S WIFE

I

My home, my lovely home, she wept
while God was sharpening his shafts
against the cities of the plain.
My mother too was called at dawn
and for me Lot's wife has her face,
the same companionable hands
touch what they shall not hold again;
it was because it meant her life
that she was loath to leave that place.

And while her daughters were already running
she stayed to look at a familiar sight:
flowers responding to the early sun
– the valley emulated Paradise;
sweet view, she sighed, if I could leave my eyes . . .
no one will love you after I have gone.

II

What was she doing, waiting there
with darkness spattering the air;
don't hang your hearts on things, she'd said:
a nomad used to moving on
with only a shabby, a makeshift home
and daughters who still needed her
hurrying ahead?

III

I'd be content with yesterday, she thought,
her memories like clothing in her hands:
her daughters small, herself reckless and young,
and Lot her shelter, and their wanderings.
If God must take, she thought, let him take all . . .
and shivered as the ground began to shake.

BABY MARY

I

When did the choice of her begin,
was she marked out when she was born,
Jesus shining from within
the baby on her mother's arm,
or was she like her sisters and brothers
to anybody except her mother?

II

Men worship the invisible
– the mother sang a lullaby –
my temple is this miracle
so fragile in her tyranny.
Nothing the corn knows in the seed
of the hunger it shall feed;
little Mary, be my bread.

III

No more than trees that give their fruit
can mothers do, the woman thought,
kissing the pollen from the skin.
I cannot spare her anything
for all the care I wrap her in.

IV

A well in the desert is my daughter,
King Solomon's ships she is to me;
I have a hosanna in my cradle,
sang the woman in Galilee.

V

From all the earth, from all of time
thoughts of people must have come
like gifts to make that baby strong.

MILK AND HONEY

I

Those who were children in the wilderness,
future soldiers and the sons of slaves
– you'll be God's gardeners, their mothers said –
have-nothings, became scavengers of words.
If one began, When we came out of Egypt . . .
they were like livestock at a water-hole.
They tamed the desert with the things they heard.

II

Having kept vigil for the spies' return,
they were the front-ranks squatting at their feet;
they saw the pastures flowering with meat
and fruit like coloured lanterns in the trees
and giants guarding their inheritance;
but they could not imagine so much green.

They did not stay to hear the arguments;
they called out, milk and honey, like a name,
they called it out till it became a chant,
and while their elders shouted, back to Egypt!
the words took hold of them and made them dance.

III

Imagine them grown gaunt with deprivation,
imprisoned in the furnace of God's hand,
until there was a whole new generation
for whom the desert nomads' tents were home.
Still they said, milk and honey, to each other:
a password meaning, we shall reach that land.

RACHEL'S DEATH

I

They were not very different from us.
When Joseph cried all night long for his mother
– too young to understand that she was dead –
a woman like myself who held him close
whispered to him, love your baby brother.

To get some light she opened up the tent
– that desert view would become Bethlehem –
and felt her breath snatched by the browsing stars.
Perhaps she prayed, Great Shepherd, if you are,
let me atone for what you did to them.

II

Barefoot he squatted beside the baby.
When he fed Egypt and was alone,
all the treasure of the Pharaohs
was dross by comparison.

III

Sundry mothers in the tribe
nursed the baby while the boys
held each other with their eyes.

Repetition makes a rope
of the gossamer of touch;
the new-born did not miss her much.

Out of the granaries of grief
Joseph provided for his mother
as none of us with equal love
have for those who gave birth to us:
an oasis of compassion
where all children mourn together.

THE DEATH OF KING DAVID'S BABY

I

When they showed him the child he roared with laughter
– all others had been beautiful and strong,
Does this do justice to my greatest passion?
Is this her homage to a warrior king?
and saw their hooded eyes like snuffed-out candles
and muttered, but the boy has done no wrong.

II

Are you so tame, he taunted death,
    that you must feed on crumbs?
Tell God to find me enemies
    and let you feast on men!
But he was on that battlefield
    where none is champion.

III

Hands that had caressed and killed
held the baby patiently;
he thought, what good is my crown to me,
they call me the father of Israel
and I can do nothing for my own child.
The little God asks is all he has;
an early death is a stopped-up well
and he might have watered the wilderness.

IV

Hushed were palace and city
while the king was shut up alone,
for seven days and seven nights
he prayed to save his son,
and the dust came out of the desert
to darken Jerusalem.

V

I have lost my war with death, he said,
        should I now war with life?
It makes no difference to the dead
        whether or not we grieve,
and clapped his hands for the servants
        to bring him wine and meat.

INTO EGYPT

I

Trading in spices, once they bought a slave;
not something they remembered and retold,
but into Egypt was a longish way.

They must have made sure he would not escape.
Roped to a camel by his wrist or waist,
was he their equal or an animal;
did one abuse him and another say,
he will recover and can still be sold?

II

Bold were the stars like the eyes of his brothers,
far were his dreams like his father's tents;
night herded child and strangers together
as the desert stampeded before the wind.

III

Perhaps they tamed him as they went
with stories of huge monuments,
water as wanton as the sun
and green fur covering the plain
and towns exuberant with men.

IV

Later, they liked him better than their own:
a mascot with sweet pastures in his head;
I see him burning, bird-boned, gently bred,
beguiling twenty brigands with his dreams.
Perhaps they had agreed to take him back
– a motherless boy who made them feel strong –
and outside Egypt told him, stay here, wait;
but he had found his footprints on the track:
his children's children going the other way,
and like a prince bid them, take me along.

THAT NIGHT

I

That night they waited shut inside their houses,
fully dressed and their belongings packed;
small children lay where sleep had caught them up,
older ones watched their parents being afraid.
And then it came: a brief scream far away,
and then another, closer, and another;
a youngest child – my ancestor – exclaimed,
if they don't see the sign they'll kill my brother!

II

Where the angel went that night
the houses became loud and light;
in the slave part of the town
they stayed dark and without sound.

III

I think my mother would have said,
not at the cost of so much blood;
we shall remain the slaves of life,
better the suffering we know . . .
and would have been content enough
to weep that it was time to go.

IV

If we had been the children there
– we too went to the school of death –
we would have gone where Moses was,
enticed from our families
by promises that needed us;
we would have been his messengers.

V

In that night slavery passed like a storm;
and still, to raise what had been beaten down
needed a lifetime between dusk and dawn.

DAVID AND GOLIATH

I

Two hillsides-full of fighting men
sheathed their swords and squatted down,
grinning, to be entertained.

Even among the enemy
some did not want that fight to start;
his brothers had to be restrained.

He wasn't much to keep apart
two armies seething like the sea.

II

His mother did not think of him
as the Psalmist and future king
but as little and quick to cry,
one with imaginary fears,
the baby of the family
with scabby knees and dirty ears
and still in need of mothering.

III

You both look small in the sight of God,
sang the brook to the boy picking stones;
the water that yields to your hand
makes wadis when it is in flood;
you took on the world when you were born,
you can be a giant without big bones.

He must have thought that victory complete:
manna of peace falling throughout the land
and no man dying until he was old,
during that hush before the roar began:
one army fleeing and one in pursuit.

CAIN

I

What made me think he did not grieve?
He killed his brother and left home;
the wilderness took back his fields,
his parents thought of other sons;
he had nothing and was alone.

II

All things looked at him with his brother's eyes,
the younger one to whom he was the source;
all creatures he encountered went in pairs,
the stronger as dependent as the other;
the echo of his senses was, his brother.

III

Gentle must have been his hands
coaxing produce from the land,
that could be so violent.

All the slow builders, time and men,
    are quick to destroy;
only what is over remains
    unchanged, perpetually.

LEAH

I

How could she, lying nightlong in his arms,
have fooled her bridegroom with her sister's name?

He must have known his Rachel was not this
reluctant body with averted face
stampeded into passion by a kiss.

For seven years, dull in her sister's shade,
her love had been about him like a slave.

All night she dithered between dread and bliss.

II

She wasn't of those for whose sake
the oceans cleave the continents
and miserable men are brave
and pregnant women count the days
and ecstasy bides in the skin.

III

Warm from her bed he went where Rachel wept.

She picked up garments he had shed in haste,
six tribes in her and barren in the heart.
With such a margin has the world been made,
her lavish love is lost among the waste.

URIAH THE HITTITE

I

Straight out of battle to Jerusalem,
God's promontory with the feel of home
– children at play and old men gossiping
and miracles like bunting in the streets –
he came, one of King David's mighty men,
with quickened eyes and music at his feet.

II

They were waiting for him, his cinnamon girl
and, blinding him like sunshine, the young king
– who would have gone unnoticed in a crowd;
exhausted, grimy, thinking of war he stood
friendless before his best-loved enemies.

III

On wings the day rose as he parted from
the shepherd city dancing through the hills,
the warrant for his death against his heart;
the road rolled up behind him as he went
and in a distant fortress the blithe sun
gilded the sword by which he would be killed.

SAUL AT EN-DOR

I

Who leads the leader? the king exclaimed,
his army outnumbered, war declared,
God silent and his prophet dead.
He laid his royal cloak aside
– and was at once like other men –
and secretly, disguised, by night,
sought out what was lying in wait for him.

II

Not with tree stumps but the dead
was that hill afforested;
dew-ponds mirroring the moon
were the eyes of his three sons;
loudly went the Philistines:
their trophy was his cloven head.

III

The kingdom's greatest warrior stood
abject in the witch's hut
and saw the spectre of her look.

IV

Head and shoulders above his men
he went into battle and was brave;
not any hope of victory
but being human drove him on.

Additional Poems

PROGNOSIS

I

Part of my future I know:
arthritis will cripple my hands,
my spine if I live to grow old;
to admit it is not the same
as having been told.

What frightens me has a name.

Such knowledge we share in vain,
within my skin I am alone.

II

The burning child I was
remains unreconciled
to making do with less
than once seemed possible:
no relationship whole,
no poem saying enough,
nothing as I imagined it,
all life at the mercy of
being randomly spoiled;
with my crooked fingers I write:
I am not reconciled.

III

I don't know what it's like for them,
it's an experience I lack;
my adult children coming home
have feelings I have never had:
when I was their age my parents were dead.

Part of my future is plain:
I shall grow dependent on others;
what is it like for children
to have to look after their mothers?
And what might make my family
decide to let strangers look after me?
Will anything I do or don't do
make them make strangers look afterme?

V

Suddenly they are everywhere,
old women who need looking after,
publicly chewing the cud of their troubles.
(Old woman, what is it like for you
to have become your daughter's child?)
She was never like me and I won't grow like her.
(Why does the street beset me with mirrors?)
When I am her age I'll not be as old.
(All around me potential doubles.)
I'll not let one of my daughters become
servant to an old woman like them.

VI

When I was their age and alone,
without family, without home,
my childhood harvested like corn
stored away and I unfed,
when no one cared what became of me,
I learned to care about others instead;
yet long after my first children were born,
when asked about my family
I would answer, they are dead.

VII

For twenty-eight years I have woven
my children's lives and mine
into a cunning tapestry
each has for his own;
it has a shifting centre
time must take me from.

FIRST MEETING

I

While you sat talking I was not listening:
I would have liked to have taken the short-cut of touch,
not for the sake of physical satisfaction,
but to break through what separated us
to what we have in common, and to reach
further into your life than I could with speech.

II

Accepting me on sight, you took me through
your life as if it were an exhibition:
I am committed to you because I looked,
caught in a battle that is past for you
as if I could bring about a fresh decision.

III

If this were the beginning of a story
we would have been invented as we are;
co-operate with me to turn the page:
before we will be changed to fit the ending
let us rebel against it and celebrate.

SILENCE

As life needs water I need words
to make my feelings come to heel,
while you keep silent when you feel;
I've learned not to appeal to you
so that you will approve of me
more constantly than I would love.

GROWING OLDER

I cup my hands to keep life whole,
burned to the bone by what I'm holding;
growing older I cannot let go:
I am possessed by what I own.

WORLDS

That girl you looked at carelessly
also ferments in the veins of life;
think how the sun has laboured for her sake,
what species, empires were melted down
to make this jewel. Perhaps other planets
dismiss the earth as you dismissed her face.

THE PAST

As salt in the sea
the past in us is,
as sight is in eyes
it lies in the memory;

who would wish
the mind a cure
like that of the flesh –
to be as before?

Joshua Poems

THE ANNUNCIATION

Captive in fear or dream she lay,
the angel was part man, part bird,
a searing sunburst were the words
that took her maidenhood away;
her mother, at some early chore,
saw no more than a curtain stir.

The morning came like any other
with the old sun and the usual weather;
the girl got up to her mundane day
bearing no mark of special grace:
an ordinary human face
was what she could be distinguished by.

She walked through Nazareth uncrowned,
unnoticeable in a crowd,
tawny-skinned and elfin-boned,
desert honey in her eyes;
clutching the bunch of prophecies
engendering within her womb
the martyr's cross, the empty tomb,
was she disconsolate or proud?

GOING TO BETHLEHEM

As they were going to Bethlehem
– a week it took in the winter rains,
avoiding the Legion and common dangers
by keeping to secondary lanes –
the couple were still almost strangers;
sad and silent the child-bride was,
uncomfortably near her time;
delicately stepped the ass.

Humbly her husband walked beside her,
also a Joseph who was a provider;
perhaps he was, like her, quite young:
an averagely sensual man,
who cursed his luck as they plodded on,
certainly thought that she had done wrong
and – brooding jealously on the other,
dreaming of harm he could save her from,
of being barbarous and strong –
behaved as if he were her brother.

Such innocents to guard the birth
that farmed the spheres to feed the earth!

CHRISTMAS

It was not as we think of it,
a welcome refuge for the night,
romantically candle-lit;
the air was foul and misty with
the warm breath of the animals
champing and stamping in their stalls,
and even while fresh straw was spread
it was trampled in the mud;
a weeping wind drove through the walls
rain and the sound of revellers;
I know in those days people were
less squeamish and still primitive
but it was a degrading place:
no wonder she thought it a grace
to see the baby born there live.

THE BIRTH

As if the prophecies were beasts
she held her son against her breast
pleading, Joseph, be my shield,
turn them away and let me rest;
he's not exceptionally made
and nobody has any proof,
I don't care if the world is lost,
say it's a girl to keep him safe.

Dark was the grotto, dank and bare,
her motherhood filled it with light;
the dialogue of earth and sky
was like a multitude outside.
How dare I challenge fate, she thought,
what fortress does my love provide?
and cowering from wings called out,
behold my son! into the night.

THE SHEPHERD

One who was left behind to watch the sheep
was so despised that he's not in the story;
a cripple or too old to leave the field,
a misfit or a sceptic or a fool,
or else a desert-hatched and desert-hardened
berry of a boy kicked out of sleep.

Alone in the flittering night with the fidgety flock,
the sky above Bethlehem awash with glory,
did he cower among the beasts not to venture his life?
I think that he stood as if challenging lightning to strike
– as the first men to know themselves human stood
        upright with pride –
and sent forth the dove of his imagination to look.

THE WISE MEN

Those were not presents for a child;
a clamorous and callous dream
put gold and incense in their hands
and sent them off to Bethlehem
where lay in his cocoon of joy
the honey-coloured dimpled boy
too fast in life to understand
the prophecy these men fulfilled.

THE FLIGHT INTO EGYPT

They set out as it was getting light
– food in the kitchen, the beds unmade,
some of the baby clothes not dry;
he'll miss his playmates, Joseph said,
handing to Mary the sleeping child,
not hesitating in the flight
that would get all those babies killed;
and was some angel haunted by
the act of waking him that night?

Though manna fell for them like dew
and clouds of birds tempered the sun,
they asked as the desert went on and on
– as exiles no longer in danger do –
perhaps what we are escaping from
is no worse than what we are going to?
and knowing through what a little tear
the spirit can spill from the skin
said, death can find him also here.

In the teeth of despair they stumbled on
a pagan trading caravan
– princes to these refugees;
desert-tamers who thought them mad,
with their towny ways and their talk of God
and their claim that they were not alone,
but did not move and made no sound
when the baby quiet on the ground
brought all the camels to their knees.

THE BETHLEHEM BABIES

All the babies were killed – imagine it happening:
the knocking on the doors perhaps at dawn;
from breasts, from cradles, from the beds of siblings
the soldiers picked the fruit for their terrible wine.

Or did they cunningly invite the mothers
to bring their babies to the market square
– some fathers could not keep their toddlers back;
perhaps an orphan brought her little brother –
and did those first in line not warn the others
because the truth was more than they could bear?

Later, strangers found that age group missing;
there was a rumour of an infant plague,
started when officials came to count
the mess of bodies in the common grave.
Local people knew that one escaped
and nightly women dreamed, that one is mine.
Oh, long before some said that Christ had risen,
all the Bethlehem babies had risen in him.

OUT OF EGYPT

Where everything he saw was home
he poured his look out like the sun,
making the flowers turn to him
and lizards start from under stones;
when he came out of Egypt and
his bare brown boy's feet touched the land
it shook the hills of Lebanon.

JESUS AS A BOY

How was he holy as a child
snug in an overcrowded home,
did he not snatch his share of food
or push for space to sleep at night;
was he so unlike other children
– when he got hurt he did not cry,
when he was wronged he did not fight,
when he spoke up he stood alone –
that people asked, who is that boy?

His mother looked at him and was afraid:
sometimes she saw him in a cloak of light
or was caught in the quicksands of his eyes
or in the furnace of the things he said.
At times she craved to repossess this fruit,
an unripe kernel that had sprung its shell;
while he was roaming about Galilee,
loudly singing, none shall limit me,
and wildly running with the wild gazelles.

WHEN HE WAS JOSHUA

When he was Joshua among his peers,
dark boys who dreamed of being camel-drivers,
playing in the streets of Nazareth
– green was the tree that would become his cross –
and some stray revelation sought him out,
did he reject it with, not now, not here!
flush with the body of the boy he was?

JOSEPH

The greater Joseph's love for him,
the more hurt he must have been
that the boy was not his son.

In the workshop, over some piece of wood,
their feelings tangled in a look
sadder for being understood.

Did he not flinch when someone said,
the spitting image of his dad,
and wonder whose the imprint was?

Did he never use his authority,
lose patience with the mystery
and shout, we are your family?

There must have been some moments when,
sick or tired or merely young,
Jesus said, Father, and meant that man.

CHEDER BOY

If he sat opposite the rabbi
he did his reading upside down:
a boy in cheder has his place;
when he was old enough to study
he learned to take his place among
the centuries of Jewish boys
who have no time for being young
and sometimes are killed for their faith.

VIA DOLOROSA

When Jesus walked in Jerusalem
elbow-high among the crowd,
his hand gripped by his mother's hand,
the hill was steep and narrow the lane
where his foot encountered a nugget of pain
that sang to him, I am the blood
to be shed by you when you pass again.

IN THE TEMPLE

He searched the Temple for its host.
The pilgrims went and with the day
took the festival sights and sounds away
till only the priests were left and God,
and that gossamer boy in the throes of his quest
– as seeds in the furrow were his thoughts before speech,
all his senses on tiptoe and God beyond reach –
looking as if there were two at play.

DOCTRINE

He said, the baby in the womb
knows nothing of the world to come,
perhaps death is another birth
towards which we gestate on earth.

WHEN JESUS WAS A CARPENTER

When Jesus was a carpenter working at his trade,
none thought him more than equal or revered the things he
    made.

They praised him for his craftsmanship and haggled when
    they paid,
and did not especially listen to anything he said.

Index

A Double Wedding, 85
A Jew's Calendar, 25
A Song in October, 52
After a Quarter of a Century, 98
After Auschwitz, 12
An Examination, 65
Anne in Life and Death, 20
Anti-Love Song, 94
At a Reception, 108
At Odds, 51

Baby Mary, 130
Birth, 51
By Now My Father . . ., 110

Cain (Selected Poems), 46
Cain (Coming Back from Babylon), 139
Cheder Boy, 160
Christmas, 154
Coming Back from Babylon, 128
Compared with Single Women . . ., 93
Compulsion, 105
Contact, 94

Danes Hill, 48
David and Abishag, 122
David and Goliath, 138
Death in Clapton, 106
Doctrine, 161

Easter, 18
Encounters, 70
Esther, 119
Exodus East, 39
Experiments with God, 43
Explosion, 68
Eyes, 50

Family Sum, 110
First Meeting, 147
Foster-England, 98
Fourth Child, 55
Friday Night, 34

Generations, 86
Going to Bethlehem, 153
Goodnight to Naomi, 109
Growing Older, 148

Home, 44

I Ask No Thanks, 54
I Set Out for Jerusalem, 69
I Was Not There, 7
In a Tram, 35
In Every Street, 30
In Spite of Your Riches, 53
In the Absence of Stella, 97
In the Jewish Cemetery, 31
In the Museum, 95
In the New Liberal Synagogue, 63
In the Park, 32

In the Temple, 160
In the Wood, 36
Into Egypt, 135
Israel Notebook 1966, 66

Jephthah's Daughter, 114
Jesus as a Boy, 158
Joseph, 159

Kaddish, 14
Kate's Death, 44

Late Summer, 101
Leah, 140
Lot's Wife, 129
Love Poem, 102
Love Song, 109

Married Love, 100
Milk and Honey, 132
Monologue, 33
Monologues, 59
Moses' Mother, 120
My Children Walk in
    Jerusalem, 71
My Daughter Looks at Me, 49
My Daughters, My Sisters, 92
My Father, 34
My Father's House, 89
My Mother, 30
My Sons' Brides, 86
My Two Daughters, 74

Naomi in Jerusalem, 71
Night and Day, 53
Nightfall in Jerusalem, 70
1941 and 41, 42
Noah on Ararat, 123
Notes to Carol, 73

On the Terrace, 72

Out of Eden, 127
Out of Egypt, 158

Pavements, 32
Prognosis, 145

Race, 35
Rachel's Death, 133
Ruth, 117

Samson in Gaza, 116
Sarah, 113
Saul at En-Dor, 142
Separation, 105
Silence, 148
Sometimes My Mother . . .,
    94
Songs In Exile, 8
Stella Going, 76
Stella Gone, 96
Stella Remembered, 97
Suicide, 40
Swiss Morning, 48

That Night, 136
The Annunciation, 153
The Attic, 37
The Bethlehem Babies, 157
The Birth, 155
The Children in the Street, 70
The Children's Exodus, 22
The Dead Come Back, 43
The Death of King David's
    Baby, 134
The Flight into Egypt, 156
The Past, 149
The Shepherd, 155
The Sacrifice of Isaac, 125
The Town, 36
The Wise Men, 156
Three Wishes, 53

hrough My Hands, 108
ime Which Has Made Ruins, 8
o My Children, 55
o Stella Growing Up, 95
ony, 81
ony Alone, 83
ony Gone, 82
ony in Clover, 84
ouch (Legacies and Encounters), 63
ouch (My Daughters, My Sisters), 104
ouching Flesh, 106

Touching Stella, 96
Towards Babylon, 124

Uphold Me, 108
Uriah the Hittite, 141

Via Dolorosa, 160

When He was Joshua, 159
When Jesus was a Carpenter, 161
Wilhelm Harms' House, 38
Words, 110
Worlds, 148